AMICUS HORRORS

Brian M

Kohner, Madison & Danforth

ISBN-13: 978-0-9992266-2-9

DEDICATION

To Milton Subotsky, Peter Cushing, Vincent Price and so many others all those years ago. Without their generous cooperation this book would not have been possible. Although it is sad to realize that they are no longer with us, we can be comforted by the priceless legacy they have left behind.

To my brother Paul, our childhood friend Bill Kelley and Bill's friend Christopher Lee. And to Glenn & Marghiee.

To my wife Pat, for her warmth toward Peter Cushing, her sense of humor with Vincent Price and for the constant love, encouragement and support she has given me over the years, which has brought immeasurable joy to my life.

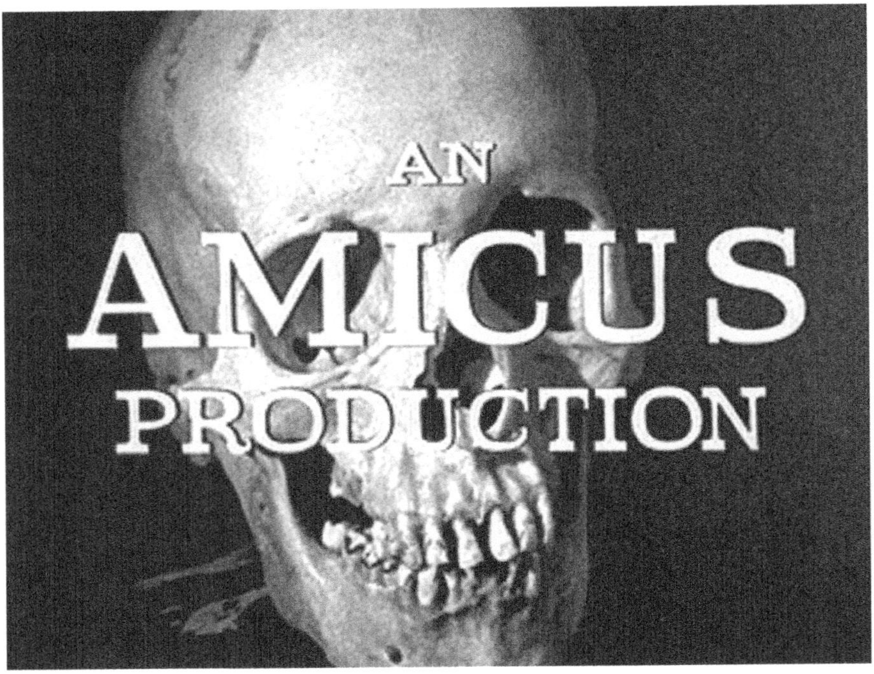
AN
AMICUS
PRODUCTION

TABLE OF CONTENTS

PREFACE

It is ironic that that one of the two film studios most responsible for the so-called "Golden Age of British Horror" was actually owned by Americans. Amicus was second only to Hammer in producing impressive horror hits, yet it was Hammer that received most of the publicity, while Amicus kept a low profile, content with high box office returns. As a young man I visited Amicus at a time when the studio, founded by Milton Subotsky and Max Rosenberg, was producing many of the best horror films to come out of Britain. I watched as some of these films were being made and spoke with the people who were making them. *Amicus Horrors* gives me a chance to share those experiences with you.

The book concentrates on the *horror* films produced by Amicus, although the studio's entries in other genres are also mentioned to give an overall view of how Amicus grew. The company's earliest ventures into rock music films receive a little extra attention here. That's because they represent the studio's first attempts to wrap a linking story around several individual filmed episodes ... in this case, musical performances. Later Amicus would use the formula to link tales of terror in its anthology films.

Milton Subotsky was always enthusiastic about discussing his work. You couldn't help but realize how much he loved making movies. And he was always welcoming, whether showing me books he was considering for future films or taking me around Shepperton Studios to discuss current and past projects. It was the same when we got together again the following year and I was accompanied by my wife. He couldn't have been nicer. And that year we got to spend some time at the other studio Milton often used, Twickenham.

With few exceptions, Amicus films had an expensive look and feel. So, on my first visit to Amicus "Headquarters" on the Shepperton lot, I was surprised to learn that it consisted of just the small wooden cabins in the background of this Vincent Price/Uta Levka publicity shot!

Amicus always used Shepperton or Twickenham, where Subotsky was completely familiar with both the facilities and the personnel. In contrast to larger film operations, Amicus remained essentially a two-man band throughout its period of greatest success. The formula rarely varied. Max Rosenberg would arrange for the financing, while Milton Subotsky would handle the production. This gave the little company a big advantage. Projects could be approved quickly without going through layers of management. And that resulted in the Amicus legacy covered in this book.

INTRODUCTION

I grew up at a time when the Universal package of legendary horror films was first being shown on TV's *Shock Theater.* Suddenly everything about monster movies was all the rage, and my brother and I joined with other kids in the neighborhood to make our own versions of *Dracula, Frankenstein,* and all our other favorites. We'd use the 8mm camera my mom and dad owned and, although the movies were silent and ran only three minutes, we were thrilled with them. And, even though we had little experience, we dreamed of one day becoming famous producers!

That's the joy of childhood ... living in a world where you really believe you can do anything you set your mind to. And maybe that's why I found myself so fascinated with Milton Subotsky, a grownup who fulfilled the dream.

My fondness for horror movies never left me, and by the time I was working for various news organizations, Britain had replaced Hollywood as the horror capital of the world. Much had been written about Hammer, but the much smaller Amicus operation was turning out some very fine films on very small budgets and I saw a story there. I arranged to go to Britain, visit Amicus and see how they did it. Milton, the company's co-founder and creative chief, was extremely helpful, spending hours with me at his home and at the studios. He also allowed me unrestricted access to people like Vincent Price and Peter Cushing.

This book provides a snapshot of a time and place that will never come again.....a London where a company owned by two New Yorkers could set up shop, produce glossy horror films with major stars, keep the budgets low, and still turn a profit. I hope you will enjoy my memories of that long ago look behind-the-scenes at Amicus as much as I enjoyed being there.

AT THE STUDIO'S CORE

Milt Subotsky was seated in his London living room, which was packed with books, scripts and film treatments. But at the moment it was clear that he considered the piece of sheet music that he held in his hand to be one of his most gratifying achievements. It was one of several songs Subotsky had written for the early rock films that he and partner Max Rosenberg produced. While the song he was showing me was hardly a classic, the very fact that it existed at all said a lot about Milton Subotsky and Amicus, the film production company he and Rosenberg co-founded. "I had never written any music before and I knew nothing about notation. But I had seen the picture *Rock Around The Clock*, and I figured I could write music just as good as the stuff they were singing, so I tried it. As it turned out, a song that I wrote for Frankie Lyman became a hit here in England and I still get royalties from it."

It was this attitude that, for the most part, served Subotsky well when he later produced a series of classic horror films on modest budgets. When he was producing a movie designed to attract teenagers, he knew he needed rock singers so he managed to sign them inexpensively. He also knew the rock singers needed songs, so he simply sat down and wrote them. It never occurred to him that he couldn't write rock music, or do anything else for that matter. And that's one of the main reasons that Amicus was so successful.

"Jungle" Sam Katzman was hardly the type of producer one would expect to inspire an intellectual film buff like Milton Subotsky. "Jungle" Sam's nickname derived from his penchant for shooting inexpensive adventure epics, like the "Jungle Jim" series, in deepest, darkest Hollywood with potted palms struggling vainly to disguise the prosaic locations. But Sam made other types of films too, and was especially adept at jumping on the latest trends well ahead of the competition. It was Sam's early entry in the Rock and Roll celluloid sweepstakes that initially drew Milton Subotsky's attention.

Growing up in Brooklyn, Subotsky had been a film fanatic since childhood. As a teenager, he wanted to get into the film business in the worst way. As it turns out, he did. It would be hard to find a job much worse than the position of go-fer that he landed with a small documentary film company. But he got enough experience to wind up in the Army Signal Corps during his military service, writing and editing training films. In civilian life, Subotsky eventually found work in very early television, and became involved with future partner Max Rosenberg, when Rosenberg distributed an educational TV project of Subotsky's that was aimed at children. If the two had continued working in television, that might be the end of the story. I wouldn't be writing this book and you wouldn't be reading it,

Instead, there was a major turning point for the company that would eventually become Amicus. As Milt mentioned, he took note of an inexpensive rock musical "Jungle" Sam had produced called *Rock Around the Clock.* True, the picture had been released by Columbia, a big operation compared to the Rosenberg/Subotsky partnership, but Columbia was considered among the weakest of the major studios. And, more to the point, Katzman really operated more or less as an independent at Columbia. Subotsky realized musicals aimed at teens presented several advantages for a small production outfit. There was no need for any big investment in sets or story, and unknown actors and actresses could play the main roles, since the only "names" necessary to attract an audience were the musical performers.

Rosenberg liked the idea and Subotsky set about

arranging for the musical acts that would appear in the film. His method for securing the talent provides an early example of the approach he used throughout his career when dealing with matters that were beyond his experience. The Subotsky motto, which he quoted to me many times, was: "Always get the best people you can within your budget." In 1956 the best authority on teen music was the man often given credit for coining the term "Rock and Roll," DJ Alan Freed.

Just as it was no accident that nine years later the credits for Subotsky's first Technicolor horror movie would read like a who's who of Hammer personnel, it was no coincidence that Alan Freed appeared in *Rock, Rock, Rock* and helped arrange for the musical acts. The script, such as it was, proved to be just an excuse to string together songs by Chuck Berry, Frankie Lymon and the Teenagers, The Moonglows, The Flamingos, The Johnny Burnette Trio and others.

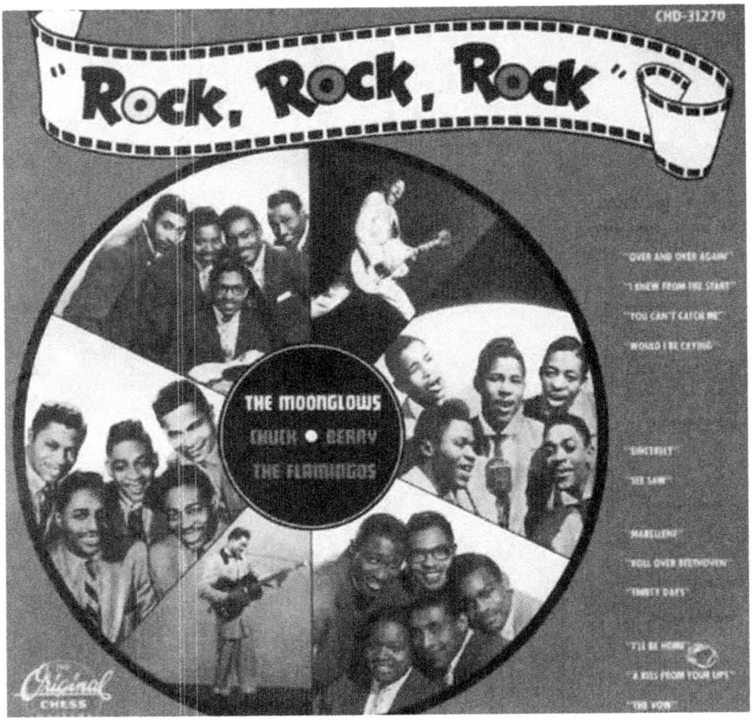

"Rock, Rock, Rock" was exactly what teen audiences wanted. The film showed a nice profit because costs were so low. Tuesday Weld was in the movie, but she wasn't a star yet, and a young Connie Francis dubbed Weld's singing voice for the film.

Columbia Pictures may have provided the proximate cause of inspiration for the New York company that would eventually become Amicus, but the real lesson Subotsky absorbed was one that American International had already been exploring on the opposite coast. A small firm could make considerable money by catering to a specialized audience consisting of newly-liberated teenagers. Best of all, this could be accomplished on a very tight budget!

Today teens, pre-teens and twenty-something's are the

main market for movies, but that wasn't always the case. Most films were aimed at adults until the fifties when a series of events combined to make marketing to a younger demographic more attractive. In the years after the Second World War home ownership in the suburbs became a real possibility for many American families. The more affluent could also afford an automobile. Cars were a luxury when living in the city. Now, helped by better roads and the migration to the suburbs, many viewed the family auto as a necessity. At the same time, cheap land and growing demand combined to make Drive-In Theaters more popular. Teenagers loved them because they were cheap ... often charging by the car-load ... and, of course, offered the perfect location for making-out. The only missing ingredient was the realization by enterprising movie-makers that it was time to target this ready-made audience.

In organizing his first rock musical Subotsky learned a valuable lesson that would serve him well when he embarked on his omnibus horror films in the future. Even with someone as knowledgeable as Alan Freed to guide him, Subotsky couldn't possibly hope to guess every act and every record that would be popular with audiences when *Rock, Rock, Rock* came out. But he could be fairly sure that a majority of them would be well received. And that, Subotsky saw, was all that was needed.

When the movie was a hit he realized that not every song had to be a winner with every viewer. If they didn't especially like one number, they didn't have long to wait until another one was up on the screen, and they'd come out of the theater with an overall impression of the film that was favorable. This realization would help form Subotsky's main philosophy toward the anthology horror films for which Amicus would become so famous. In a film like *The House that Dripped Blood,* while a viewer might not care for the comedy in the

Ingrid Pitt vampire segment, he or she might love the Grand Guignol trappings of the Peter Cushing segment.

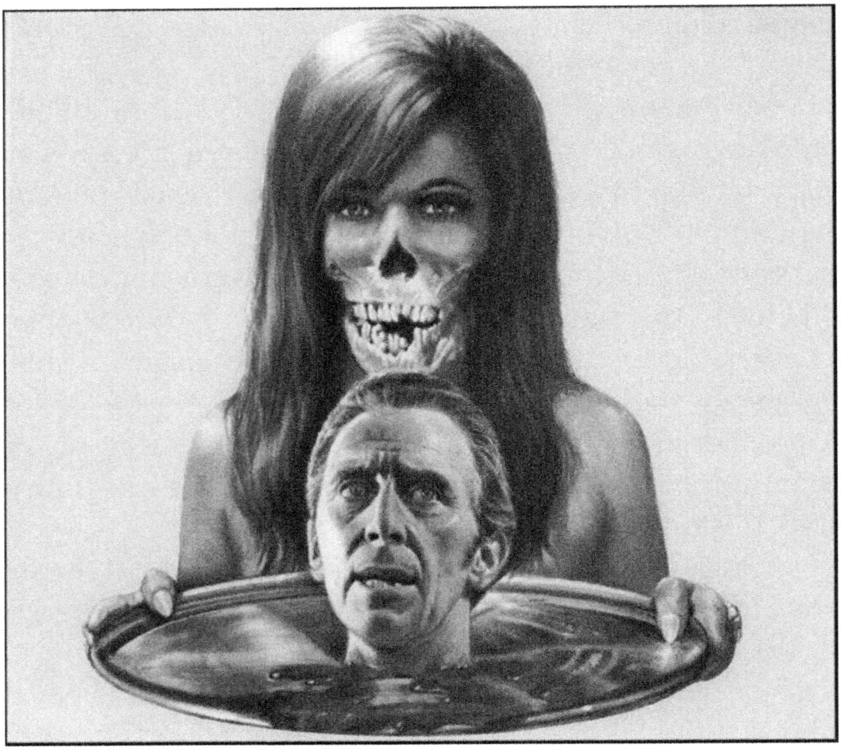

But well before they started making horror movies, Subotsky and Rosenberg were quick to try to capitalize on the success of *Rock, Rock, Rock* with a follow-up film called *Jamboree*. The movie was known as *Disk Jockey Jamboree* in England, which was actually more descriptive, since the film featured a number of popular DJ's of the time, in hopes of getting them to plug the movie on their shows. The DJ's were carefully chosen to reach the largest number of young fans. For a kid from New Jersey like me, who was located halfway between Philadelphia and New York, the film featured Dick Clark from Philly and "Jocko" Henderson from New York, who presided over "The Rocket Ship Show"

featuring the latest in rhythm-and-blues hits. Clark, at the time *Jamboree* was filmed, wasn't a national name yet. His "American Bandstand" TV show went on the ABC network around the time the movie was released.

But, as was the case with *Rock, Rock, Rock,* the real draw for most teens was the music rather than the DJ's. Connie Francis was back to do some dubbing and the acts included Fats Domino, Frankie Avalon and Carl Perkins. But the performance of the most significance to rock historians is the version of *Great Balls of Fire* rendered by Jerry Lee Lewis in the film. Jerry Lee wouldn't just lip-synch to his Sun Record's version of the hit. Instead Lewis did his own alternate take and the synch job came out looking almost live compared to others in the film. That was fine with Subotsky. Milton Subotsky trusted talented people. Years later, for example, when Peter Cushing felt he might be better suited to a different role than the one originally selected for him in an Amicus film, Subotsky went with Cushing's gut feeling.

Without *Rock, Rock, Rock* and *Jamboree* today's musical archives would be missing major footage from some of the most important acts in rock history. Rockabilly scholars are thrilled that the seminal work of the Johnny Burnette Trio was captured forever in *Rock, Rock, Rock*. And Chuck Berry's famous "Duckwalk" is preserved on celluloid in the same film.

Jamboree, meanwhile, was filled with some musical milestones too. While "Don't Want To Be Teacher's Pet," sung by a very young Frankie Avalon wasn't a hit, it did mark his first film appearance a good six years before he would begin making his "Beach" movies. Aaron Schroeder, like Subotsky a Brooklyn native, had written one of the songs for *Rock, Rock, Rock*. In *Jamboree* he made a cameo appearance playing, of course, a songwriter. Schroeder would go on to write many of Elvis Presley's biggest hits.

The teen musicals showed that Subotsky and Rosenberg had a talent for the genre and they would return to it again when they switched most production to England. Sticking with a winning formula on these early films should have been a lesson that helped Amicus later, when it sometimes stayed away from its signature horror pictures too long. Amicus was perfectly capable of doing a series of good horror films in a row...for example, *Scream and Scream Again*, *The House that Dripped Blood* and *I Monster* ... and then going entirely off the rails with an oddity like *What Became of Jack and Jill.* Subotsky would then quickly get the company back on track by producing films like *Tales from the Crypt*, *Asylum*, and similar offerings.

With *Rock, Rock, Rock* and *Jamboree* under their belts, it would have been logical for the producers to continue along the same lines. Instead, they headed in an entirely different direction. This propensity for temporarily abandoning a format they had mastered for one that might carry more prestige became a pattern with the partners, and it rarely served them well.

The Last Mile was about as far removed from the duo's rock musicals as possible. This film about death row and prison violence was well-made and even received decent reviews. But the subject matter wasn't new and it wasn't the type of movie that gave a small independent company an edge. More to the point, *The Last Mile* starred Mickey Rooney.

Years later I interviewed Rooney, but I never got a chance to ask him about the film. In fact, I didn't get a chance to ask him about much of anything because Mickey was a non-stop talker. Most of the time he was busy promoting his latest money-making ventures...I seem to recall a theme park he had in the Catskills...and I presume he needed to plug these enterprises in light of all the alimony payments he may have had to ex-wives.

Whatever the case, in the late fifties when Mickey Rooney made *The Last Mile*, he was still trying to prove himself as a dramatic actor. Some would say that in this film and in others of the period, he was trying a bit too hard. Despite the actor's best efforts, many in the audience would simply see an aging "Andy Hardy" up there on the screen.

The Last Mile was a disappointment but it didn't keep the Rosenberg/Subotsky team from considering the possibility of filming two new dramas: *Girl of the Night*, which would eventually star Anne Francis, and *Lad: A Dog*, starring Angela Cartwright.

Angela Cartwright with star of *Lad: A Dog*.

Anne Francis publicity still from *Girl of the Night*.

In retrospect, this segment of the studio's history can best be viewed as a period of biding time, until the right circumstances came into place to allow Amicus to take its rightful place in the British horror movie pantheon. When these two films came out, Rosenberg alone would get credit as producer, with no mention of Subotsky. Milton, however, wasn't initially aware of this, because he was out of the country at the time. He was in London.

AMICUS IN BRITAIN PART ONE

After the completion of *The Last Mile*, an event with enormous consequences for the Subotsky/Rosenberg partnership took place. Like most life changing events, its significance only became apparent in retrospect. At the time, Max Rosenberg's decision to co-produce a horror film with a contact in England was seen as little more than a one-off deal. Likewise, sending Milton Subotsky over to supervise was supposed to be temporary as well. But, as it turned out, Subotsky had a natural affinity for this type of film. Some years later Milton and I discussed that in his London flat.

"A horror film," said Subotsky, "is a work of the imagination designed to frighten people while they're sitting in the security of their movie seats. I was brought up on fairy tales as a child and I guess the child is still with me. I think of a horror film as an adult fairy tale. I make them for others because I enjoy them myself."

Subotsky got his first chance to try his hand at one of these "adult fairy tales" in 1959, when he began shooting *City Of The Dead* with Christopher Lee in England.

The movie, known in the U.S. as *Horror Hotel*, was shot entirely at Shepperton studios, even though it was supposed to be set in New England. Copious amounts of fog were used to try to obscure the fact that all of the "outdoor" scenes were shot indoors on a sound stage. But this actually wound up working in Subotsky's favor, adding to the eerie atmosphere of the film. Sometimes a movie works *because* of budget constraints rather than *in spite* of them.

Subotsky and Rosenberg wanted to attract both a British and American audience. To add American flavor to the film, they chose Venetia Stevenson and Betta St. John to play the female leads. St. John was born in the States and Stevenson had gone there as a child with her father who was a director and her mother who was an actress.

Venetia on the foggy Shepperton set.

Venetia was on a trip back to London and appearing on the British show *Juke Box Jury*, when she was chosen for her role in *City of the Dead.* It's just the sort of show that would have attracted the attention of Subotsky, whose main stock-in-trade up until then had been teen rock movies. Here was a lovely girl with an American accent already in London.

Venetia cheesecake publicity shot for the film.

In an interview for the beautifully restored VCI entertainment DVD of the film, Venetia gives a great explanation of how strange it felt to shoot a film set in America in Britain:

"I was born in England and I moved to America, then I moved to England where a played an American but actually we filmed it in England!"

The setting for the film is a New England town called Whitewood, an isolated community covered by swirling mist and steeped in the lore of ancient witchcraft. Forced to erect the weird buildings of Whitewood on an indoor stage with black curtains substituting for the sky, the fog enshrouded set automatically transports viewers to the kind of H.P. Lovecraft nightmare-scape that a larger production would have been unable to duplicate. The black-and-white photography only adds to the surreal atmosphere.

From the first notes of the haunting chant underneath the opening credits, the viewer knows this film is much more than a typical "B" horror movie. Just as the audience becomes absorbed in the opening flashback depicting an eerie 1692 witch burning, the scene shifts to modern-day professor Christopher Lee. It now becomes clear that the viewer has just been watching a visualization of his lecture to a group of college students. One of those students...young co-ed Nan Barlow, played by Venetia Stevenson...decides to visit the very village mentioned in Lee's Lecture, to gather more material for her studies. After ignoring warnings to stay away, Nan stops just outside Whitewood to give a lift to a mysterious character played by Valentine Dyall. He disappears from Nan's car just as she parks outside the gloomy inn where she plans to stay. Just as Dyall looks exactly the same as one of the men we've just seen in the 1692 flashback, the owner of the Inn just happens to be the spitting image of the witch we just saw being burned at the stake.

And so it goes, tensions growing as director John Moxey makes use of images as ordinary as a ticking clock and as extraordinary as the wounded boyfriend seen in fog-covered silhouette, stumbling across the graveyard with a giant cross that sets the witches aflame.

hile *City of the Dead* was Subotsky's first horror project to actually make it to the screen, an earlier idea he had for a movie helped launch The Golden Age of British Horror. Milton thought the time was right for a color version of *Frankenstein*. He and his partner Max suggested the idea to Eliot Hyman at Associated Artists (later Seven Arts.) Hyman didn't think Milt and Max had enough experience to do justice to such a project, so he sent Milt's script to James Carreras. He didn't like the script, but he did like the idea. Milt and Max got some money for their proposal, but Carreras got a blueprint for success that would make the Hammer name synonymous with horror hits and big box office returns for years to come.

So, in a sense, Milt Subotsky was playing catch-up with himself when he finally filmed his story about witches in Whitewood. In the years since, *City of the Dead* has developed cult status and much has been made of its similarities to *Psycho*. The twist of having the heroine disposed of early in the film was new and shocking at the time and it is true that the Subotsky film was released prior to the Hitchcock classic. But the book version of the Robert Bloch chiller was already creating a buzz by the spring of 1959. And *City of the Dead* didn't start shooting until fall of that year.

I can tell you from personal experience that it is virtually impossible for Subotsky not to have read the book almost as soon as it came out. One afternoon I was due to meet Milt at his flat, but he called to say he would be delayed by some last minute business at the studio. He very graciously offered to have his driver pick me up and show me various locations used in Amicus films, so that the wait would be productive. I was glad to take him up on the offer and the driver proved to be a wonderful guy. He said the only thing he absolutely *had* to do before we got back to the flat that day, was pick up the latest batch of books Subotsky had ordered. It turned out to be quite a large stack and I began to understand why Milt's flat looked more like a library. Here was a guy who simply loved to read:

"My partner and I read between one-thousand and fifteen-hundred stories a year, and if we find three good ones to turn into screenplays, we consider ourselves lucky."

Since Subotsky was big on Bloch, there's no way he wouldn't have read "Psycho" at the first opportunity. In the end, however, these "Which came first, the chicken or the egg?" questions are of more interest to film historians than they are to viewers. Who cares if Subotsky, struggling to try to extend the George Baxt screenplay, subconsciously borrowed from Bloch? Fans who've seen the movie remember only the first stirrings of impending doom and the scenes of unholy sacrifice proving those fears were justified.

Patricia Jessel and Chris Lee in sacrifice mode.

This film was a defining moment for the production company that would eventually be called Amicus. Not only did it bring Subotsky to the country that would become his base of operations, but it introduced him to the problem solving methods that would serve Amicus well as it went on to establish its reputation as a legendary producer of British horror films. And there definitely were some problems getting *City of the Dead* before the cameras.

Britain's subsidies for movie productions at the time made it an attractive place to film. Max Rosenberg, who took care of the financial end of things, knew this. He also had a contact in England, Hannah Weinstein. Weinstein was an American who left during the McCarthy era and found success in England producing the *Robin Hood* TV series with Richard Greene (who would later appear in *Tales from the Crypt*). It was Weinstein who brought George Baxt over to England. Baxt was a Brooklyn-born agent who turned to writing when business got slow, and Weinstein assigned him to write scripts for another one of her series, *The Sword of Freedom*. Weinstein at first rented the small Nettlefold Studios in Walton-on-Thames, Surrey to shoot her TV projects, but eventually purchased the facility and renamed it Walton Studios. Since Rosenberg and Weinstein were doing a co-production deal on *City of the Dead* under the Vulcan film banner, it made sense to shoot the picture at Walton. It also made sense to hire Baxt to write the screenplay. Problems developed, however, and by the time they were resolved, Walton was no longer available.

Among those problems was a script that Subotsky felt was too short. Baxt, who would soon script *Circus of Horrors* for another producer, thought *City of the Dead* was supposed to be a short "B" picture, while Subotsky and Rosenberg were planning on an "A" feature. So now Subotsky didn't have a suitable script or a place to shoot the movie. It was hardly an auspicious start for a film that was destined to become a cult classic. Even more improbable was the reputation it would develop as a *British* horror classic, given the distinctly non-British makeup of the production staff. With Subotsky, Rosenberg and Baxt working on the movie, perhaps the village of Whitewood should have been changed to Brooklyn-on-Thames.

Walton's lack of availability turned out to be a plus in the long run. Walton, which would soon be closing anyway, was extremely small. Watch any of the old *Robin Hood* shows and you'll notice how often the actors are crammed into claustrophobic sets.

Friar Tuck complains about the small studio set.

When Hannah Weinstein added additional adventure shows to her roster, she had to look elsewhere for more space. She could squeeze *Sir Lancelot* in at Walton, but she had to turn to Twickenham Studios for *The Buccaneers*, starring a very young Robert Shaw. So, when Weinstein decided she needed Walton for an ambitious new show called *Four Just Men*, she recommended Shepperton and Twickenham to Subotsky and he would use them both for the rest of his career.

The problems with *City of the Dead's* short script turned out to have a positive side too. Subotsky's "Baptism of Fire" would give him a crash course in expanding scripts and he rose to the occasion, adding additional material to the screenplay to meet the necessary time requirements. He would be called upon to do this again in future projects. *City of the Dead* turned out to be an excellent film, even under its tacky U.S. title *Horror Hotel.*

Subotsky didn't choose to capitalize on this initial horror outing immediately. Instead, he returned to the rock musical format, producing two movies in England aimed at teen audiences. *It's Trad, Dad* and *Just for Fun* were released in 1962 and 1963, respectively.

Subotsky's new base of operations gave him the advantage of being able to draw on both British and American acts. What we in the U.S. call "Dixieland" music had a burst of popularity in Britain in the late fifties and early sixties under the name "Trad Jazz." Kenny Ball who had a hit here with "Midnight in Moscow" and Acker Bilk who scored with "Stranger on the Shore" were two of the early icons of "Trad Jazz." Thus the title *It's Trad, Dad* for the first of the two British musicals. Since "Trad" wasn't a term familiar to American audiences, the film was given the U.S. title *Ring-A-Ding Rhythm.*

This title wasn't much of an improvement, though, because *Ring-A-Ding Rhythm* sounded more like a Dean

Martin/Jerry Lewis comedy or a film featuring Frank Sinatra and his Rat Pack.

Titles aside, however, once again, the plot was super-thin, the better to squeeze more musical numbers into the mix. In the film, Ball and Bilk shared billing with American acts like Del Shannon, Gene Vincent, Chubby Checker and Gary "U.S." Bonds. While combining Dixieland and Rock may sound strange from today's vantage point, it seemed quite normal to those of us who were around at the time. When the film came out in 1962, Shannon, Bonds, Ball and Bilk were all on the U.S. charts, vying with acts as diverse as Peter, Paul and Mary, Ray Charles and Chubby Checker.

But the movie had more going for it than just the fact that the acts it featured were so popular. It also had a director, Richard Lester, who would go on to become a motion picture icon.

***Trad/Ring-a-Ding's* Helen Shapiro & Richard Lester**

Milt Subotsky was familiar with Richard Lester's work from two short films he'd shot in England. One was on jazz, and the other was a slapstick comedy. The comedy featured members of "The Goon Squad," a kind of early "Monty Python" ensemble that included a young Peter Sellers. Subotsky felt Lester, who like himself was a transplanted American, might be just the right person to helm *It's Trad Dad.* Working on the film, Lester honed the frantic style of unusual camera angles, speeded up action and intercut shots that would be praised as an innovation when he directed *A Hard Day's Night* with the Beatles in 1964.

Milt Subotsky wrote some of the songs for *It's Trad, Dad!*, as he did for all of his teen musicals, and the fact that he was able to do so was quite impressive. The one possible drawback, however, was that he remained fascinated with pop music and at times inserted it into films where it wasn't appropriate. As will be discussed later, *The Deadly Bees* really could have done without a performance by the British group "The Birds." It's not that they weren't talented ... guitarist Ron Wood would later join the Rolling Stones ... it's just that a rock number seemed out of place in the movie. Even in a film Subotsky made on his own years later, *The Monster Club*, the songs are a bit jarring. Music belongs in this one, since the framing story is set in a disco. But tunes like "Sucker for Your Love" in a movie where Vincent Price is a vampire, are a bit too obvious even if the film is supposed to be a comedy.

It's Trad, Dad made a handy profit. But in a virtual repeat of what happened with *Rock, Rock, Rock* and *Jamboree* back in the U.S., Subotsky's second teen effort in England, *Just for Fun,* wouldn't prove as popular as the first. It wasn't for lack of some good music, however. The film featured plenty of well-known talent, including American artist Bobby Vee singing one of his major hits, "The Night

Has a Thousand Eyes."

So what went wrong? For one thing, Richard Lester was no longer in the director's chair. But another development that would limit the film's appeal had actually taken place well before the movie even went into production. Brian Poole and the Tremeloes, who appear in *Just for Fun* because Amicus used acts from Britain's Decca Records label for the film, had won out over another group in competition to be signed by Decca. The other group had been nervous at their Decca audition and failed to impress the powers that be at the label with their performance of mostly cover versions of older songs. Decca executives felt, not unreasonably, that the public wasn't exactly clamoring for a band that performed chestnuts like "Besame Mucho" and "The Sheik of Araby." However, the group, then known as "The Silver Beatles," subsequently tightened their act and, as simply "The Beatles" *did* win a contract with Decca rival EMI.

The upshot of all this was that, when Subotsky raided the Decca stable for musical talent, most of the acts he got for his film were about to be swept away by Beatlemania. Amicus had, in addition to Bobby Vee and Dusty Springfield, Freddy Cannon, Ketty Lester, The Crickets and Johnny Tillotson in the movie. But by the time *Just for Fun* came out, The Beatles had begun their phenomenal climb in Britain with early hits like "From Me to You" and "Please Please Me." Had the Beatles signed with Decca, who knows? The entire history of Amicus might have been different. The company could well have continued to concentrate on catering to the youth market with teen musicals. Luckily for those of us who love horror films, that was not to be.

Also on the plus side for Amicus fans, *Just for Fun* introduced Milt Subotsky to the advantages of shooting at Twickenham Studios, which would serve as a base for some of his future endeavors in the horror field. Richard Lester, by the way, would shoot "A Hard Day's Night" at Twickenham and he maintained an office at the studio for many years.

But Milton Subotsky, as we mentioned earlier, would decide to set up his offices at Shepperton, where he had filmed *It's Trad, Dad.* Among the advantages that Subotsky found both studios offered, even at this early date when he was still shooting musicals, was the availability of useful locations nearby. For example, Amicus saved time and money by shooting some of the scenes for *It's Trad Dad* just two miles from Shepperton at Sunbury-on-Thames, where it was easy to get a small-town feel by filming on local streets and a more sophisticated backdrop by concentrating on area office buildings like the British Petroleum Center.

But beyond making Subotsky more comfortable with the studios and technicians Amicus would use in future films, the teen musicals would play a major role in the evolution of a format for which the small production company would become most famous. Through these inexpensive little musical marathons, Subotsky got his first real experience with multi-segment movies. Back then he was writing scripts to tie several musical numbers together. Later he would use much the same technique in the omnibus horror films that became the Amicus trademark. Instead of weaving various songs around a single theme he simply combined several tales of terror into a horrifying whole. Subotsky's first attempt at doing this, *Dr. Terror's House of Horrors,* was a winner and paved the way for a series of similar films that will be discussed in the next chapter.

Dr. Terror's House of Horrors provided the template that Amicus would use to develop a style of its own. Others would try to duplicate it, but none would be as successful.

AMICUS IN BRITAIN PART TWO

Milt Subotsky had long been nurturing the idea of turning several short stories into a fantasy film. Subotsky's preference for multi-story shockers came from his own love for the legendary British film *Dead of Night*. The movie provided a template for Subotsky's later films by successfully linking several unconnected stories through a single narrative. Most viewers remember the best known segment of the film about a ventriloquist who thinks his dummy is alive. But Subotsky remembered the movie's overall formula and stored it away for use at a later time. That time came in 1964 when, as mentioned earlier, Subotsky began work on *Dr. Terror's House of Horrors*. The linking device was a simple one. Several people, including Chris Lee, meet the mysterious "Dr. Schreck" (Peter Cushing) on a train, and he tells their fortunes with Tarot cards.

Since "Schreck" is German for "Fright," it should come as no surprise that their fortunes are less than cheery. The film was a major success, helped by the fact that two of the biggest horror stars of the time, Peter Cushing and Christopher Lee, appeared in it. This was the first time that Amicus would shoot a Technicolor horror film that could be considered competition for Hammer's product and it's an excellent example of the approach Milt Subotosky emphasized in our conversations. If he knew how to do something he did it. If, however, he needed help, he went out of his way to get the best people possible given the limitations of his budget.

The polished look that has led casual viewers over the years to confuse *Dr. Terror* with a Hammer production is no accident. It certainly helped that Milt Subotsky hired Freddie Francis to direct.

Freddie Francis, Christopher Lee and Milt Subotsky.

There were other Hammer connections in addition to the presence of Cushing, Lee and Francis. *Dr. Terror* had Bert Batt on board as assistant director. He had worked on *The Devil-Ship Pirates* and *The Gorgon.* His other Hammer films include everything from *The Curse of the Mummy's Tomb* to *Dr. Jekyll and Sister Hyde.* Assisting Batt *on Dr. Terror* was Hugh Harlow who went back to the earliest days of Hammer horror, beginning his career with the company as a teenager. Harlow had been on hand for *X The Unknown* and *The Curse of Frankenstein* and was still working at Bray Studios when *Rasputin* was filmed back-to-back with *Dracula Prince of Darkness.* He had just begun freelancing when he took the *Dr. Terror* assignment. Subotsky also hired Harlow's wife, Pauline, another Hammer regular, to handle continuity on the picture. Also adding to the Hammer feel was makeup master Roy Ashton. He would continue doing makeup at Amicus through *Vault of Horror.*

Roy Ashton makeup for *Vault* publicity shot.

Ashton had worked on virtually every major Hammer horror, beginning as an uncredited assistant on films like *The Curse of Frankenstein* and *Horror of Dracula*. Ashton was even joined on *Dr. Terror* by Hammer hairdresser Frieda Steiger who'd been teasing tresses at Bray since *The Brides of Dracula*.

Music on the Amicus film was provided by Elisabeth Lutyens who was responsible for the soundtracks for Hammer's *Never Take Sweets from a Stranger* and *Paranoiac*. Meanwhile, Alan Hume, who had been Director of Photography on Hammer's *The Kiss of the Vampire* performed the same duties on *Dr. Terror* and would work on future Amicus productions like *From Beyond the Grave*.

Subotsky quickly followed up *Dr. Terror* with another Cushing/Lee pairing in *The Skull*. Freddie Francis was back at the helm and the screenplay was based on a Robert Bloch story.

The only problem with *The Skull* was that the script came up short. But Francis and Subotsky provided extra scenes that added the necessary time and even earned praise from some critics.

After a brief detour into sci-fi territory with *Dr. Who and the Daleks*, it was back to Bloch for Subotsky's next horror offering, *The Psychopath*, once again directed by Francis. There was plenty of atmosphere and a seasoned cast but no big name stars. Instead *The Psychopath* relied on character actors like Patrick Wymark and the film did only so-so business.

Amicus then took another brief break from Robert Bloch to mine *Dr. Who* territory once more. The first film was a success so it just made sense to do a sequel. *Daleks — Invasion Earth 2150 A.D.*, once again featured Peter Cushing. This second *Dr. Who* outing didn't fare quite as well as the first one, but the box office returns were still fairly impressive in Britain.

Next, Amicus turned to Robert Bloch again to do the screenplay for *The Deadly Bees* and brought Freddie Francis back to direct. There are many reasons a film can go wrong and critics have cited most of them at one time or another in connection with *The Deadly Bees*. But a basic choice made early on in the film's planning stages certainly contributed to its failure.

If you're going to shoot a movie where much of the action takes place in a farmyard, make sure you film it at a studio that has a big back lot. That's the one thing Twickenham did not have, so the "farmyard" was constructed on a sound stage, giving *Bees* an overly theatrical look. In addition, to say the superimposed swarms of bogus bees were unconvincing would be an understatement.

Suzanna Leigh pretends she's afraid of fake bees

There were two more Amicus disappointments, *The Terrornauts* and *They Came From Beyond Space*, both forgettable sci-fi sagas suffering from terminal cheapness, before Amicus decided to return to its winning omnibus format.

Torture Garden had Burgess Meredith handling the framing device chores and featured Peter Cushing in one of the stories. Others in the able cast included Jack Palance and Hammer veteran Michael Ripper, who had also appeared in *The Deadly Bees*. *Torture Garden* did fairly well, and ended what was beginning to look like a losing streak for Amicus.

Since *Torture Garden* helped Amicus get back on track,

it might be well to pause here and consider the many benefits that the anthology format held for Amicus. The most obvious plus, which Milt Subotsky was quick to point out, was the fact that it saved on star salaries. If a big-name actor appears in only one of the several stories in an anthology film, he may be needed for only a few days of shooting.

"We always try to get absolutely the best cast we can for all of our films," Subotsky told me. "We can do that because we schedule very tightly and very carefully. This way we get people coming in for one, two or three days, and shooting all of their material."

Cushing and Palance in their *Torture Garden* story.

Subotsky said that carefully going over the schedule with an eye toward the budget helped in other ways too, when it came to cutting costs without sacrificing quality. He gave me the example of a movie that originally called for filming on location on a Sunday. Subotsky realized it was the only filming that would be done that day, and it would have meant calling in an entire crew that would have to be paid at the overtime/weekend rate. By rescheduling the scene, he was able to save quite a bit of money that could be used to better advantage elsewhere. Going over the script with a fine tooth comb to cut costs required a great deal of pre-planning, but during my visits with Milt Subotsky I came to realize that careful planning was one of his strong points.

As we rushed between his flat, his office at Shepperton, the sets at Twickenham and various locations, he somehow managed to keep track of two films that were being shot simultaneously and one that was in post-production.

Milt making a point on location

To save money on his films, Subotsky took on much of

the work himself. He said he wanted the money Amicus spent to show up on the screen, not in executive salaries. Subotsky put it very simply:

"We take the profits and we pump them back into Amicus. The more money we make, the more money we pump back into the company. In the long run it pays off, because we make quality pictures."

And that's one of the main reasons that Amicus was so successful. Subotsky didn't have a lot of money to spend, so he decided to do much of the work himself. The money that was saved could be pumped into better production values. There was, of course, a downside to Subotsky's willingness to take on so many jobs. As Amicus' success grew, so did its production schedule. At times, Subotsky would be trying to supervise pre-production and post-production on as many as three films simultaneously. It was virtually impossible to juggle that many films without something falling by the wayside, but his overall track record was remarkable.

It also appeared to me that Subotsky enjoyed wearing so many hats on these films because he simply loved the movie-making process. That message came through loud and clear in his overwhelming enthusiasm. One day, when I called Subotsky's office his secretary told me he was somewhere on the Shepperton lot, but she wasn't sure of his exact location. She said he was just finishing editing the film *Asylum*, the Amicus follow-up to *Tales from The Crypt*, and was getting it ready to be shown to financial backers. Later, when we met at his flat, I learned Subotsky was also busy going over books and screenplays for possible future projects. It became obvious that Subotsky viewed film making as both a business and a labor of love.

Nothing had changed the next time I visited Amicus. Milt was shooting two films at the same time at two different studios, and working on pre-production for a third movie.

And once again, it was clear he was happy being so busy because he was doing something he really enjoyed. He was proud to show me where he had shot his films, how he had shot his films, the scripts he had written for his films and the stars he had hired for his films.

Subotsky reminded me again that he could afford those stars because he would often carefully schedule them for only a few days of work. A major star like Sir Ralph Richardson might only be needed for the linking scenes in an omnibus film and his scenes could be shot in a day or two. Someone like Christopher Lee might appear in only one segment of an episodic film, and his presence might be required for only a few days.

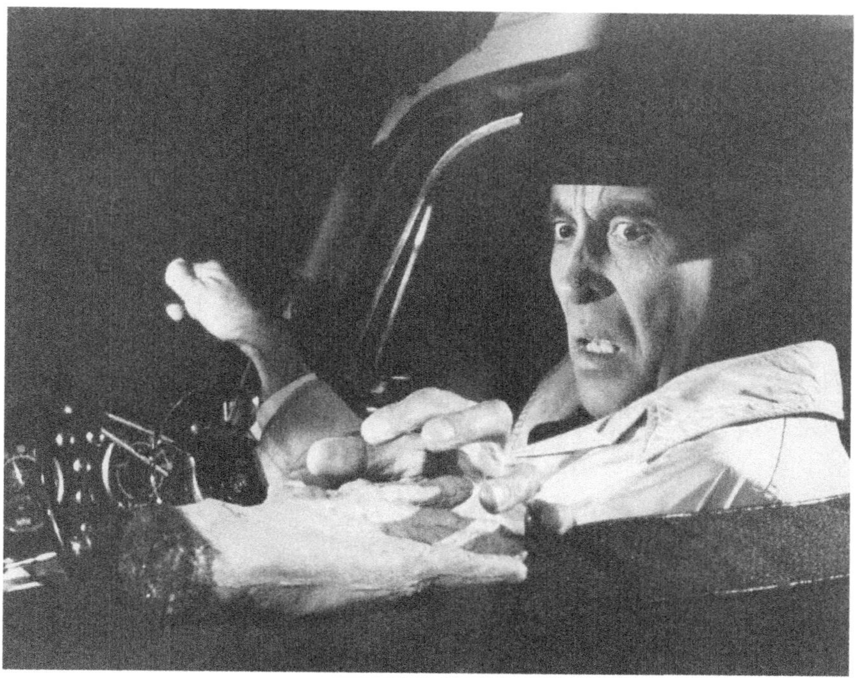

Lee's segment in Dr. Terror's Housel of Horrors

And the savings for Amicus went beyond the lower total expenditure when paying stars on a per-diem basis. Milt

Subotsky was a film fan who had also worked in early television. And early television borrowed some techniques from the "B" films of the thirties and forties. Re-lighting a set, bringing the cameras back, and making sure everything is exactly the same as when the last scene was shot all takes time. Shooting all the scenes that took place on a particular set at the same time saved a tremendous amount of money on set-up costs, a fact that was quickly realized by the producers of "B" films and serials.

The practice carried over into early TV. A show like *Superman* filmed all of the "Perry White" office scenes for several episodes at once; then the crew would move to "Clark Kent's" office and film all those scenes at once. It meant the scripts for several shows had to be ready ahead of time, but it was well worth it to the producers. This, of course, was economy carried to the extreme. In the case of a film like *Dr. Terror's House of Horrors*, since Peter Cushing appears only in the train sequences, it was an easy matter to film those sequences all at once and simply insert them throughout the film. But savings on set-ups and salaries weren't the only benefits of using the omnibus format, according to Subotsky.

"It's very hard to sustain a single story over 90 to 100 minutes, which is the length of most films today," Subotsky said. "With a multi-story film we can tell four or five stories with no fear of boring the audience. If one particular story isn't as good as another, then the audience says, 'Oh well, we'll wait this fifteen minutes or so and we'll be into another segment.' If we shoot the film and find that one of the stories doesn't work all that well, we can cut it down so that it runs only about a reel rather than three reels."

Like the "B' movie-makers of old, amicus also employed actors who needed a first break as well as those who already had names in the business but were going through a lull in their careers. In both cases, Amicus knew it could get value for the money. A young Donald Sutherland may not have been well-known when he appeared in *Dr. Terror's House of Horrors*, but he was an excellent actor.

Likewise, Richard Greene may not have been at the peak of his career, but his presence added marquee value.

One final money-saving trick from old Hollywood that didn't escape Amicus was the re-use of sets from more expensive films. Most of the "B" movies of old had an expensive look because they borrowed sets from "A" pictures. So when the "B" unit at 20th Century Fox turned out pictures like the horror film *The Undying Monster* and *The Man Who Wouldn't Die*, an entry in the Michael Shayne detective series (both 1942,) the lavish set originally constructed for the Basil Rathbone/Nigel Bruce *The Hound Of The Baskervilles* (1939) was re-used. It was the same at RKO, Universal and other major studios as well.

While Amicus didn't own its own studio, Subotsky chose Shepperton as his base of operations, a studio that was big enough to have standing sets and its own backlot. When necessary, Amicus could take advantage of existing sets and props. This gave the Amicus product a more expensive look, while at the same time saving money.

Now that we've outlined the economic advantages of the approach Amicus took to its horror films and most especially to omnibus offerings like *Torture Garden*, it becomes even harder to explain why the company did a total turnabout on its next three films. *Danger Route* was a spy movie that didn't fare too well, while *The Birthday Party* and *Thank You All Very Much*, known in Britain as *A Touch of Love*, were more prestigious pictures. *The Birthday Party*, especially, appeared to be an attempt to emphasize the "CLASS" in the reputation for "CLASSic horror" Amicus had at the time. Even the company's next attempt at Sci-Fi, *The Mind of Mr. Soames* proved to be too up-market to attract large audiences.

Subotsky never brought up these films in our talks, and I never asked him about them. After all, my main interest was the company's horror film output. And the movies Amicus shot during this period certainly didn't fall into that category.

The first out of the gate was *Danger Route*, a spy thriller with a good cast. It was a little different from its competitors at the time because it offered a cynical look at the spy business. But you wouldn't know that from the advertising, which was aimed at James Bond fans.

If *Danger Route* was a little unusual for Amicus, then *The Birthday Party* was a total journey into uncharted territory. Turning a play ... especially a play like this one ... into a motion picture is rarely an easy task. And, to nobody's surprise, there were problems.

Director William Friedkin was a driving force in bringing the play to the screen and he had some definite ideas on how it should be presented. And he was apparently far from diplomatic in the way he expressed them. He made a very good film but reportedly alienated almost everyone in the process. Friedkin hadn't yet won the acclaim that would come with *The French Connection* and *The Exorcist*, but his work here foreshadows his future success. And the cast, led by Robert Shaw, was excellent.

Patrick Magee (who would appear in several other Amicus films,) also gave a powerful performance. Unfortunately, *The Birthday Party* failed to score at the box office. Although well done, the film's subject matter had little appeal at the time.

But Rosenberg still hadn't given up on prestige films. For his next production he chose to bring the Margaret Drabble novel *The Millstone* to the screen.

Called *A Touch of Love* in Britain and *Thank You All Very Much* in the U.S., the film was about a student who gets pregnant and chooses not to marry the father, but to live alone with her child instead. The different titles didn't seem to do the movie much good. Neither did the impressive cast headed by Sandy Dennis as the pregnant young woman. Also featured was Ian McKellen, making his screen debut.

A young Ian McKellen with Sandy Dennis

Perhaps because of the disappointing results from its most recent films, Amicus decided it was time to tackle a science fiction project that would presumably have more widespread appeal. But even with this movie, *The Mind of Mr. Soames,* the subject matter was more cerebral than fans had come to expect. It was a good film, with an excellent performance by Terrence Stamp, but to many it seemed that Amicus had lost its way.

Finally, in 1969, the company got back on the horror film track. Deke Heyward, who originally helped me get in touch with Milton Subotsky, worked for American International. A.I.P. had Vincent Price under contract and Milt had a book under consideration as a possible film project. Deke and Milton got together and the Amicus/A.I.P. co-production, *Scream and Scream Again* began shooting in the spring. Bringing together Price, Christopher Lee and Peter Cushing for the film proved to be a novel idea, although it was disappointing to learn how little screen time Lee, and especially Peter, actually had in *Scream*. When Milton told me he occasionally was able to use a big name for only one day of shooting, I believe he had Cushing's appearance in this film in mind.

The brief presence of Cushing and Lee (not even in the same scenes) could almost fall into the category of "Guest Appearances" on *Scream and Scream Again*.

Lee is seen twice in an office setting. In one shot he's addressing other men and in the second shot he's speaking on the phone. We also see Lee walking around Trafalgar

Square where he meets a foreign intelligence operative played by Marshall Jones.

Lee does, however, get one chance to shine at the end of the picture, when he uses his hypnotic "Dracula" stare to back Vincent Price into a vat of acid! Price was the only one of the big three who had a decent amount of screen time in the film.

Despite a disjointed script, *Scream and Scream Again* did quite well and Amicus was quick to follow it up. It wasn't lost on Amicus that a return to horror also marked a return to better box office results. So why not revisit the multi-story format that worked so successfully for *Dr. Terrors House of Horrors* and *Torture Garden*?

Robert Bloch wrote *Torture Garden* and more of his stories were mined for *The House That Dripped Blood*, with the author providing the screenplay as well. The house itself was the actual framing device, which proved to be a rather ingenious idea. *The House That Dripped Blood* is one of the best of the Amicus anthology films, with Christopher Lee and Peter Cushing in excellent form. It has the added benefit of a fantastic performance by Jon Pertwee, one of the actors who played "Dr.Who," and it also features the lovely Ingrid Pitt.

Pertwee holds "Curse of the Bloodsuckers" script

Whether worrying about the script for his latest film, "Curse of the Blood Suckers," or complaining about the cheesy sets and embarrassingly bad makeup, Pertwee is at his comedic best. Peter Cushing is also excellent in his segment, playing a man who has never gotten over his long lost love and is shocked to find an image of her in a wax museum.

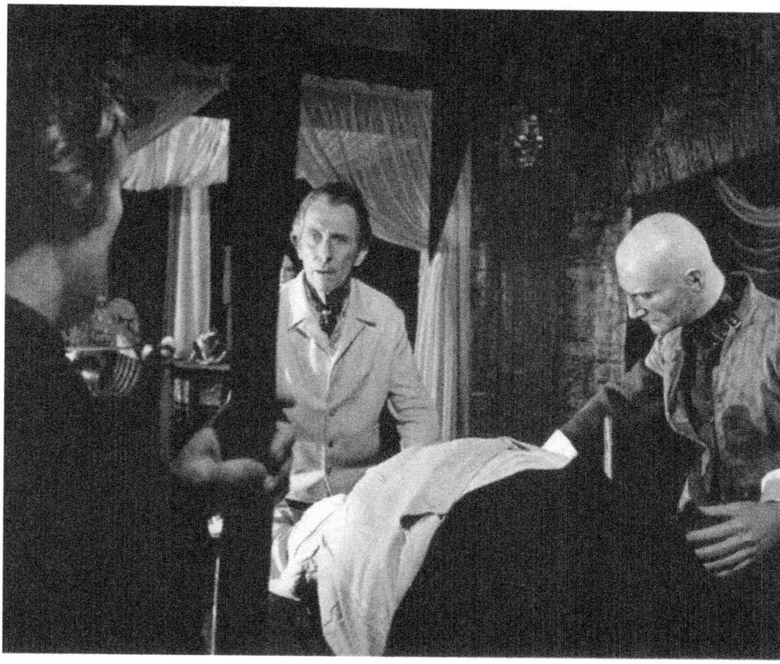

The House That Dripped Blood was filmed only two years prior to my first visit to Amicus and I had seen it when it first came out. I told Milton how impressed I was with the film, especially with the sinister brick "House" of the title and with the mysterious wax museum featured in the Peter Cushing segment of the movie. Subotsky laughed and, since we were on the Shepperton lot at the time, he took me over to see the original *House That Dripped Blood*. Later, I'd get a chance to visit *Jacqueline's Museum Of Horror*, where Peter Cushing finds himself obsessively attracted to one of the wax figures. Both locations will be discussed later in the chapter on Shepperton. Suffice it to say here that neither was even remotely what they seemed in the film!

One day Milton was kind enough to take my wife and I

on a tour of the back lot at the studio Amicus called home. Among the most impressive sets at Shepperton was the huge London Street originally constructed for *Oliver*. The movie had been shot prior to my meeting with Subotsky, but the set was still standing and it had served Amicus well in its production of *I, Monster*, starring Christopher Lee and Peter Cushing.

I hadn't seen the movie yet, but between the very impressive looking sets and the fact that an actor of Lee's talents would be playing the plum part of a Jekyll/Hyde-type character, I assumed *I, Monster* would be one of the best Amicus movies ever.

But there was something I didn't know at that time, and Milton didn't bring it up on that bright, sunny day at Shepperton. It turns out that he originally wanted to shoot the film using a 3-D method he was convinced would work well. However problems developed while the film was underway. There were questions about the constant camera movement required for the process from the young director Stephen Weeks and even from some of the actors.

Peter Cushing, Chris Lee, Director Stephen Weeks.

As it turned out, the movie was released "Flat." That makes some of the camera movements that were used to accommodate the original 3-D process look a bit strange when *I, Monster* is viewed today.

If you go on the internet and do a search for "3-D without glasses" you'll come up with brief examples of a technique that, although not the same as the one Subotsky wanted to use, works on a similar principal. They each use constant movement to create the 3-D effect. The method Subotsky wanted to use required more fluid movement and a dark lens over one eye. In both cases, though, the trick is that one eye processes the image more slowly than the other. That's why, in *I Monster*, the camera is constantly panning.

These days, when I view the movie, I try to concentrate on the performances of Chris Lee and Peter Cushing, which are quite good, while attempting to ignore the constant camera movement.

Despite problems with certain films, though, by this time Amicus had a reputation for making above-average horror movies and, as Peter Cushing told me, that assures you of a certain built-in audience:

"I think the only thing you can liken these pictures to is the success of those wonderful Hollywood westerns. No matter where you go in this world, there always seems to be an audience for these films."

For some reason though, before returning to the genre, Amicus took another ill-advised detour with *What Became of Jack and Jill.* The film, about a young couple out to murder grandma, wasn't really a horror movie or a mystery.

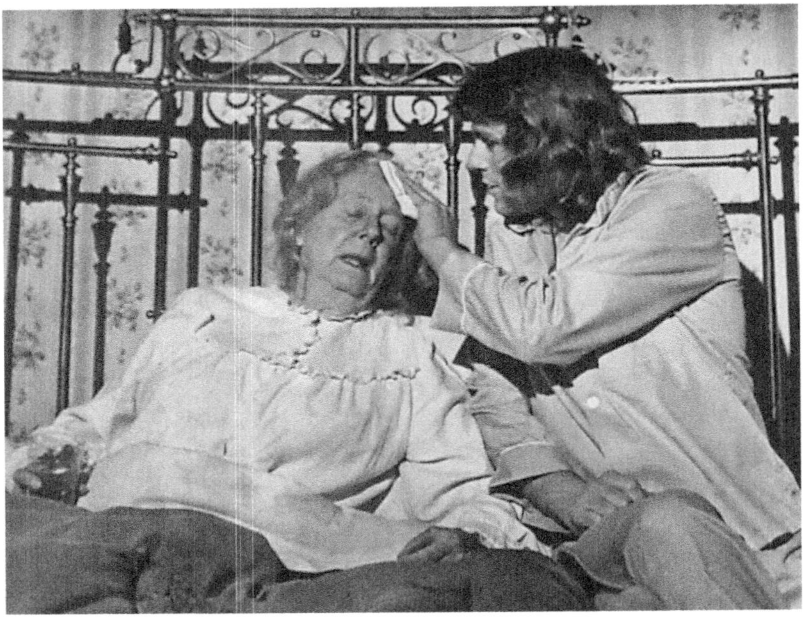

Mona Washbourne, Paul Nicholas in *Jack and Jill*

And Jack and Jill didn't fall into other categories either. It wasn't a teen musical because the jarring music was mostly in the background and there weren't lots of groups performing lots of hits. And if it was supposed to be a youth message movie it failed, because the message was murky and depressing. The film's performance at the box office was, not surprisingly, disappointing.

On the plus side, Amicus wasted little time in getting back on track. *Tales from the Crypt* was based on the EC Comics series, with Milt Subotsky writing the screenplay. As mentioned earlier, Subotsky told me he was quite pleased to get someone of Sir Ralph Richardson's stature to take part in the framing story, where he plays The Crypt Keeper.

While Richardson was certainly a prestigious name, the rest of the cast was none-too-shabby either. Peter Cushing, Patrick Magee, Robert Hutton, Nigel Patrick and Richard Greene were all on hand, along with Joan Collins in a far from heartwarming holiday story about a murderess in fear of a sinister Santa. Again, Subotsky had arranged their schedules so that he only needed them for a matter of days, not weeks, keeping a lid on the budget.

When I first met Milton Subotsky's driver, I asked him which of the many stars he chauffeured around was his favorite. He immediately said it was Peter Cushing. "That Mr. Cushing, he's quite a guy. He was sitting yesterday, just where you're sitting now. I've driven him many times. He's a real gentleman." The driver explained he'd taken Cushing out to the studio the day before to a post-production dubbing session for *Asylum*. As usual, Subotsky had assembled a talented cast. In addition to Cushing, the film featured Patrick Magee, Herbert Lom, Robert Powell, Barbara Parkins, Britt Ekland, Sylvia Syms, Charlotte Rampling, Barry Morse and Richard Todd.

Richard Todd plays a naughty husband.

Once again Robert Bloch wrote the screenplay, but Subotsky turned to veteran Hammer director Roy Ward Baker to helm the movie. It was unfortunate that I had arrived just a few days too late to watch shooting of the film, because *Asylum* was a movie that I really enjoyed when I finally got to see it. As a consolation prize for not being on hand to watch the movie being filmed, Milton gave me a copy of the original *Asylum* script, one of the few screenplays that Amicus shot pretty much as written. Robert Bloch was happy about that, but ... over the years ... said he was quite unhappy that Subotsky had changed the order of the stories as he had presented them in the screenplay. It turns out Bloch had the creepy asylum attendant Max take Robert Powell's character (named "Foster" in this preliminary script) to Bruno the tailor first.

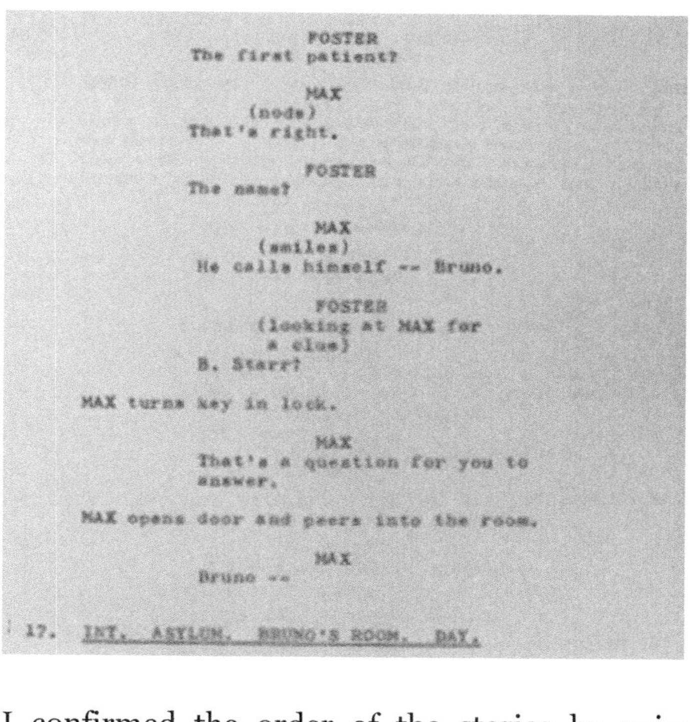

FOSTER
The first patient?

MAX
(nods)
That's right.

FOSTER
The name?

MAX
(smiles)
He calls himself -- Bruno.

FOSTER
(looking at MAX for a clue)
B. Starr?

MAX turns key in lock.

MAX
That's a question for you to answer.

MAX opens door and peers into the room.

MAX
Bruno --

17. INT. ASYLUM. BRUNO'S ROOM. DAY.

I confirmed the order of the stories by going to the original script Milton had given me (above.) I found the bound document on one of my bookshelves next to a dusty press kit for *The Revenge of Doctor Death.* I had always assumed that what I had was the shooting script for *Asylum,* since I hadn't looked at it since before the film was released.

Instead, it turned out to be the original screenplay that Bloch had supplied to Subotsky. It confirms that Bloch planned to begin the film with "The Weird Tailor" segment which would eventually star Peter Cushing and Barry Morse. He wanted "Lucy Comes to Stay" with Charlotte Rampling and Britt Ekland to be the second story, and "Frozen Fear" to be the third. In both Block's script and the finished movie "Mannequins of Horror" with Herbert Lom was the last story in the film. Subotsky decided to make "Frozen Fear" the first story, kicking off the anthology with a more shocking tale than "Lucy Comes to Stay." Bloch thought that was a mistake. He deliberately wanted to start the film off slow and then have it build.

Subotsky decided to forego the anthology format and turn to straight gothic horror for his next film, *And Now the Screaming Starts!*

Roy Ward Baker was back in the director's chair and Peter Cushing and Patrick Magee were among the returning actors. They were joined this time around, by Ian Ogilvy and Stephanie Beacham. The screenplay was by Roger Marshall, who had written the script for *What Became of Jack and Jill* two years earlier. The film also starred one of my favorite horror locations, Oakley Court, which I made it a point to visit.

The author at film location Oakley Court.

The beautiful manor house, which became a luxury hotel, sits on the Thames not far from the old Bray studios, and was frequently used by Hammer.

And Now the Screaming Starts is a gothic piece complete with spooky family plot.

And Peter Cushing sports a period hair-do that's a little hard to get used to.

Subotsky's next move made perfect sense. Since *Tales from the Crypt* had done well, it was only logical to once again visit EC comics, this time for a film version of *Vault of Horror*. As was the case with *Tales from the Crypt*, Subotsky would write the screenplay. But there were some differences too. Freddie Francis had directed *Tales*. Roy Ward Baker would take his place on *Vault*. The cast for *Tales* had, as already mentioned, been particularly impressive, featuring Sir Ralph Richardson, Joan Collins and Richard Greene in addition to Amicus regulars such as Peter Cushing and Patrick Magee. *Vault* had Daniel and Anna Massey, Terry-Thomas and Glynis Johns, Curt Jurgens and a pre-*Dr. Who* Tom Baker, but there were no really big horror names.

A rope trick turns deadly for Curt Jurgens

The fact that the film was shot at Twickenham rather than Shepperton is another minus. Other than the opening shot of office buildings in London, the only outside shots are right in Twickenham and in nearby Richmond-upon-Thames, which I visited with Milton's driver. Everything else is stage-bound, including a very unrealistic tropical island in the Tom Baker segment of the picture. On the plus side, Subotsky wrote the screenplay from original EC Comics stories and a couple of the segments are excellent. The vampire story *Midnight Mess* heads the list.

By this time, Milton Subotsky had been going pretty much non-stop. Between the fall of 1971 when *Tales from the Crypt* began shooting, and my next visit to Amicus in Spring of 1973, Subotsky had wrapped production on four horror movies, writing the screenplays for two of them. On my arrival, I found Amicus had two additional films before the cameras and a third in pre-production. It seemed to me that most of the day-to-day details of making these films fell into Subotsky's lap.

Despite the pressure of wearing so many hats at Amicus, I only saw Subotsky lose his temper once in the time I spent with him. It happened during this 1973 visit to Amicus. Milton and I were out at Shepperton's screening room, watching the unedited footage from the previous day's shooting on the film that was then known as *The Revenge of Dr. Death*. I remember the scene well, because I was sitting in the back of the darkened room feeling sorry for myself. We were watching a group of extras playing reporters, gathered around Vincent Price and eagerly asking him questions, as he exits a ship. Why, I thought, hadn't I come down a day early and perhaps been included among the extras? As I sat there lost in thought about missing my "Big Break," I realized there were a great many shots of the same scene with Price and the reporters.

Some were in extreme close-up, others were from a great distance. I suddenly heard Milton Subotsky, who I had come to think of as "Mild-Mannered-Milt," go ballistic! Subotsky was complaining that, in some shots you could almost count Vincent's nose hairs, while in others you could barely make him out!

Seeing the movie today the sequence in question appears as a brief medium-shot of Price surrounded by reporters, so taking it from so many different angles may not have been necessary. But there are two sides to every story. The man who was coming in for all the criticism was Jim Clark, director of the film that would eventually be released as *Madhouse*. Clark undoubtedly thought he was playing it safe by giving Subotsky a wide range of shots from which to choose. Or it may have been that Clark was just tired, at this point, of what he viewed as Subotsky's interference. Milt, however, viewed it as a waste of time and a waste of film, and he made that known in no uncertain terms. In an excellent interview published in the October 2000/January 2001 issue of *Filmfax*, Jim Clark told author Johnny Meyers that he and

Milton essentially weren't speaking by the time the picture was finished. Clark told Meyers:

"I don't know how to describe Milton, really; he was an absolute pain in the arse, but there was a part of him that I liked. He was enormously enthusiastic."

Jim Clark eventually decided he wasn't all that happy with being a director, but he continued to work as a well-respected film editor who was very much in demand. He served as editor on, among others, *Marathon Man* in 1976 and *The Killing Fields* in 1984.

Even as *Madhouse* was being shot by Clark, filming was underway on *Tales From Beyond the Grave*, later to be called simply *Beyond the Grave*. It starred David Warner, Ian Ogilvy and Donald Pleasence, with Peter Cushing as an antique shop owner who foresees the fate of customers who cheat him.

Former editor-turned-director Kevin Connor was at the helm for this one. His promotion worked out so well that

Amicus would use him for several of its later films as well.

As mentioned, Subotsky also obtained the services of some of the more established horror directors too. Hammer's Freddie Francis worked on several of the best known Amicus films, including *Dr. Terror's House of Horrors, The Skull, Torture Garden*, and *Tales from the Crypt*. The talented Roy Ward Baker was another Hammer director who worked at Amicus, turning out films like *Asylum, And Now The Screaming Starts*, and *The Vault Of Horror*.

Subotsky wrote scripts for some of the Amicus films himself, but he used outside talent for others. As already pointed out, the most notable writer in that category was Robert Bloch. It was another indication of Subotsky's determination to get the best talent possible whenever the budget allowed. It's ironic that some of Subotsky's scripts came in for such criticism over the years from people like Freddie Francis and *Scream and Scream Again* director

Gordon Hessler. I don't think Milton necessarily considered screenplays his strong point, but I can honestly say I never knew anyone who felt more passionately about the importance of the script. Back when I first met Subotsky I asked him the standard question you always ask someone in the movie industry: "What advice do you have for young people who want to get into the business?" His answer surprised me.

"I know this is a generation that is very cinema-minded. But I would advise anybody who wants to be involved with movies to study writing and literature. Writing is crucial to movie. A good picture always starts with a good script. The reason there aren't better movies is that there aren't enough good script writers around."

Subotsky told me a first-rate script always attracts the best actors:

"The only way to get the big names is to have a script they really like. It's awfully important to get a good script. You get the top stars only in cases where you've got an intelligent script. So, in pictures like *Tales from the Crypt* we could get somebody like Sir Ralph Richardson. Now, he certainly doesn't need the money. He just liked the script and agreed to do the part. In the film *Asylum*, we got Herbert Lom, Peter Cushing, Patrick Magee, Barbara Parkins and Barry Morse. Again, they just liked the script and agreed to do the parts."

It's probably no co-incidence that the first script Milton mentioned to me was for *Crypt*, which just happened to be written by Subotsky. But, to be fair, he also mentioned the Robert Bloch screenplay for *Asylum*. Moreover, at least whenever I spoke with him, I never got the impression of a man trying make a big deal out of his contributions to the company's success. And he definitely did have a talent for getting big names to appear in his movies.

Certainly the films I watched being shot had no lack of star power. In addition to Vincent Price and Peter Cushing, *Madhouse* featured Robert Quarry, Adrienne Corri and Linda Hayden. *From Beyond the Grave*, meanwhile, starred Cushing, Donald Pleasence, Ian Bannen, Ian Carmichael, Nyree Dawn Porter, Diana Dors, David Warner, Ian Ogilvy and Lesley-Anne Down.

Ian Ogilvy and Lesley-Anne Down

Unfortunately, not all that long after my second visit to Amicus things began to unravel. Within two years, Milt Subotsky would resign from the Amicus board, amid infighting and differences with Amicus co-founder Max Rosenberg. Milt's name would appear on a couple of additional Amicus films that were in the works, but he would soon be on his own.

Made while the Subotsky/Rosenberg team was coming apart at the seams and extending into the period just beyond the rupture, *The Land That Time Forgot, At the Earth's Core,* and *The People That Time Forgot* satisfied the youthful audiences they targeted.

Viewed today, however, these films offer little to those who aren't devoted fans of Doug McClure (and he's really just a guest star in *People,*) or obsessive connoisseurs of mediocre special effects. On second thought, though, there is the nostalgic value of seeing movies that we found magical at the time. And, for those of us who are still kids at heart, I suppose that's not too shabby!

There were a couple of similar films made after Amicus fell apart. Kevin Connor co-produced and directed both *Warlords of Atlantis* and *Arabian Adventure.* However, these films weren't as successful as their predecessors.

Although Subotsky would soon make another omnibus film, *The Uncanny,* (1977) which he co-produced with a Canadian company, things just weren't the same. The film was shot in Canada and not even the presence of Peter Cushing and Ray Milland could save it. Young Chloe Franks, who had appeared in *The House That Dripped Blood*, *I Monster*, and *Tales from the Crypt*, was also in the cast. Yet, for reasons that will be discussed later in this book, the film was a failure. There was a segment featuring Donald Pleasence and Samantha Eggar that was rather good, but overall the film lacked the old Amicus magic.

Pleasence and Eggar in *The Uncanny*.

Soon Subotsky had a new company with a new name, "Sword and Sorcery." It was an unusual logo for a film company or anything else at the time, because that particular subgenre of the fantasy-adventure novel was just beginning to catch on with the general public.

In 1979, Subotsky co-produced the film *Dominique*

under the Sword and Sorcery banner. It had an excellent cast, headed by Jean Simmons and Cliff Robertson. There were guest stars galore as well, including Flora Robson and Ron Moody. Yet, for reasons that will be discussed later, the film was a failure.

Milton gave the anthology horror film one last try in 1980 with *The Monster Club*, a movie with Vincent Price and John Carradine that was mostly played for humor.

Milt Subotsky was involved in several other projects as well over the years. But when he passed away in 1991, he was still best-known for the glory days of Amicus. I was always grateful that I had the chance to visit Amicus and get to know Milt during that creative period. I suppose that's why I look back on it all as a magical time.

In later years, after Milton Subotsky and Max Rosenberg split, Rosenberg sometimes claimed that his contribution to Amicus had been underestimated. I can't pretend to know anything about this because I never met Rosenberg. But then, neither did some of the people who appeared in his films. Ingrid Pitt is a case in point.

In the February 12, 2009 issue of the British newspaper *The Guardian*, Will Hodgkinson quotes Ingrid Pitt, who starred as a sexy vampire in *The House that Dripped Blood*:

"Rosenberg, who was the money man, was always in America and we never met him ... but Milton was an angel.

He was often on set and he had a way of making you feel wanted."

While some say Subotsky was too "hands-on," insisting on too many re-writes and re-edits, the man I saw never asked others to do anything more than he demanded of himself. Milt Subotsky was an unusual combination of movie fan and movie executive. I admired his enthusiasm and I don't believe there could have been an Amicus Studios without him.

PETER CUSHING AT AMICUS

Peter Cushing looked older than I had imagined and rather frail. Later, I would find out why. But for now we were simply discussing his distinguished career, as he relaxed between takes on a new film. The famed British actor had an unusually long break between set-ups because his stunt double was working on a scene in which Cushing, fighting with Vincent Price, gets stabbed by actress Adrienne Corri, tumbles over a banister and falls into a spider terrarium.

Peter and spiders under glass.

The movie they were shooting at Britain's Twickenham Studios was called *The Revenge of Doctor Death*, but would eventually be released as *Madhouse*. It was a bit of a madhouse on the set now, as the crew tried to arrange cardboard boxes in such a way as to safely break the fall for

Peter's stuntman. The boxes would be enough to do the trick because the distance between the banister and the terrarium was in reality quite small.

In the finished film the camera angle and wide lens would give the impression that the drop was huge!

Inventive camera angles, carefully written shooting scripts and well-designed sets that could double for more than one location were just some of the tricks that Amicus used to make its budgets stretch. In some ways, Cushing told me, Amicus was a bit like Hammer, the studio that first made the actor a horror icon with the 1956 film, *The Curse of Frankenstein*.

Peter Cushing being interviewed by the author.

"Hammer had a great deal of success by leaving leeway in both their budgets and their schedules," said Cushing. "For example, suppose they said 'You've got a thousand pounds to make this picture.' It meant there was another five hundred in the kitty to offset other things. And if they said, 'Right, you do it in four weeks,' it really meant five. It was a very clever mental approach, giving them one week under, knowing it was quite safe for the production to go the extra week, and it worked beautifully. In the end, they nearly all took five or six weeks."

Both Amicus and Hammer limited their films to a certain budget and a certain schedule. And Hammer would never strike a set until they had gotten maximum use out of it!

"It helped," said Peter, "that they were able to use the same sets over and over again with no one really knowing the difference. While a keen eye would notice the sets weren't always completely revamped, I think it was a very good economic measure."

Like Hammer, Amicus found ways to keep costs to a minimum, yet still have its pictures look sumptuous. Cushing said Hammer had one big advantage there, and his name was Bernard Robinson.

"He was one of the outstanding members of the Hammer team. You know how, if you're having your house painted, they set up scaffolding? Well, he built scaffolding both on the lot and inside the sound stages. He did it in such a way that you never had to take down the essential structure. You would just revamp it, adding a bit here, subtracting a bit there. But the whole major structure remained."

While Amicus used standing sets at Shepperton Studios and nearby real locations for exteriors, Hammer was confined mostly to the Bray lot in the early years, but Cushing said the same tendency to economize prevailed: "We didn't bother much with exteriors on *Curse of Frankenstein*, and one of the first times we used Bernard Robinson's scaffolding outside was, I believe, in *Horror of Dracula*. We used it for the outside of his place and then it was turned into Baskerville Hall for the Holmes picture" (*The Hound of the Baskervilles*, Hammer, 1959.) "Of course, it was only a skyline, so you never had to bother about telephone poles sticking up or anything like that. The scaffolding was just a shell and as soon as you went through the door you'd cut, and we'd be inside the studio doing the interior scenes. That saved quite a bit of money."

The picture below shows Castle Dracula being revamped into Baskerville Hall and you can see the scaffolding Peter talked about at the top.

Amicus co-founder Milt Subotsky used a variant of Hammer's practice of re-using the same revamped sets again and again. Subotsky would try to arrange for the use of expensive sets from other films that could be reused with minimal changes, giving his own movies a much more expensive look. Cushing felt such money-saving measures made sense. "After all," he said, "it's the stories and, I hope, the actors that count."

As we sat on the sound stage, waiting for Peter to be called for the next scene in this American-produced film, Cushing talked about his first attempts to attract the interest of studio executives in America. "I went over there in 1939, with absolutely no idea that there was a war brewing, let alone going on. I was so single-minded about my career that I never noticed other things around me. Anyway, I sort of worked out what to do when I got to the states. I went to the New York offices of the major studios and they were very kind. I got introductions and advice. They said if I was going to go to the coast, I should just go for a sort of holiday. Of course, they couldn't know that I was absolutely without money. But I was determined to get into pictures."

Cushing did manage to make it to the coast, and while he hardly took Hollywood by storm, he did get parts in a few films. Cushing said, even though no one actually saw much of him in his first movie, the experience he gained was invaluable. "I pushed out to Hollywood and used my introductions. One of them led me to Edward Small's studio ... I don't think it exists anymore ... where James Whale, who strangely enough did the original *Frankenstein*, was directing a film with Louis Hayward."

Hayward played twins in *The Man in the Iron Mask*. Cushing explained they wanted someone to play opposite Hayward, while he reacted in shots that would eventually give the impression that the two twins were talking to one another. Cushing said it was made quite clear to him that, except for a very small bit part, he would not be seen in the final print. "I knew I would be cut out of the film. They simply thought it was unfair to have Louis Hayward playing to nobody," said Cushing.

"They literally cut the two bits of film up the middle, threw my bits away, and stuck the Hayward shots together so he wound up playing opposite himself. But it was great to get the part. I had never stepped inside a film studio, knew nothing about the medium or what to do. And it was such an advantage to learn from the great stars that were in the film

... Joseph Schildkraut, Joan Bennett, Warren William, and Alan Hale. To have learned from such professionals was anyone's dream. I was on the picture for about two months and I learned a great deal from them."

Peter then landed roles in other films. He appeared in the Laurel and Hardy comedy *A Chump at Oxford* and had quite a good role in the Carole Lombard movie *Vigil in the Night*. There were other films around this time too. A rarely seen MGM short contains one of his more interesting, although brief, performances. Peter, who was 27 years old, plays young Clive of India.

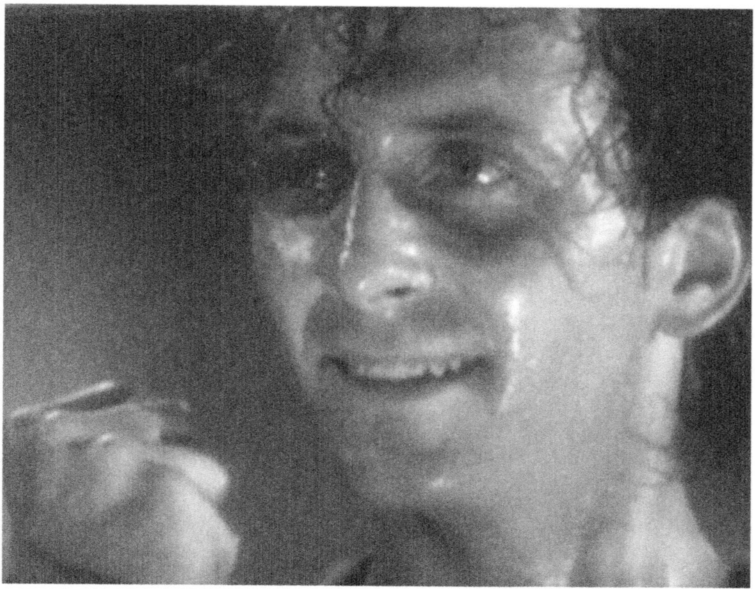

A "Eureka" moment for Peter as Clive

Ironically, this 1940 MGM *Passing Parade* short about the role fate plays in life foreshadowed the omnibus films Peter would do for Amicus decades later. There were three different stories featuring three different actors with a common theme linked by a narrator.

Peter would be the narrator in his first film of this type at Amicus, the very successful *Dr. Terror's House of Horrors.* Providing the template for the other anthology movies that Amicus would make, several individual stories were held together by a single framework. In this case Peter, as the *Dr. Terror* of the title (or more precisely, Dr. Schreck,") used Tarot cards to relate the tales of passengers on a train. This is one of those films where the little extras Peter adds to his performances, are a joy to behold. Notice the little bits of "business" ... the way he plays with his monocle and his watch, the way his hands, wrapped in fingerless gloves, caress the Tarot deck. And Cushing is perfect as he deflects the insults of pompous art critic Christopher Lee. The two were reunited the next Amicus film, *The Skull.*

Peter had the larger share of screen time in this one, while Lee's role was more of an extended guest part. So, once again, Subotsky's practice of saving on star salaries kept production costs low.

Another way to save money on a movie was to have a built-in audience so you didn't have to spend as much on promotion. Hammer had done it by making screen versions of several television shows, and Amicus decided to do the same with a big screen version of *Dr. Who*. Peter appeared in *Dr. Who and the Daleks* in 1965. It was a success, and he was back the following year for *Daleks – Invasion Earth 2150 A.D.*

Peter Cushing with Jill Curzon

In late 1966, Amicus began production on *Torture Garden*, a return to the anthology horror format. However this time around, Peter wasn't the central player in the framing device. Burgess Meredith did the honors, while Peter was featured in the story *The Man Who Collected Poe*.

Peter's role in *Torture Garden* would be a lot larger than his screen time in his next non-anthology horror film for Amicus. *Scream and Scream Again* has the distinction of featuring three top horror stars, made possible by the Amicus penchant for scheduling actors so that their services were required for as little as one day. While Vincent Price and Christopher Lee have more substantial roles in this film, Peter Cushing gets killed early on.

As was the case with most of the films Peter made for Amicus, the rate per day was good, but the number of days varied.

"It's an odd thing, but audiences never seem to resent the sort of life that they like to imagine actors live, which of course, I certainly don't. One would think people might be unhappy because of high salaries. But audiences today never seem to say 'Why does he get so much.' I think they know that, unless an actor is under contract, and there are very few actors under contract today, the job he's on now may well be his last for a very long time. I've gone for two years without sight or sound of a job. And an actor is often getting paid by the day, so it's a very uncertain profession."

There was nothing uncertain, however, about the fact that Amicus would continue to seek Peter's services for its films. His professionalism and name value were, by this time, part of the Amicus formula for success.

Cushing made two films for the company in 1970, both with fellow horror icon Christopher Lee. The one in which they actually shared substantial screen time was called *I, Monster*. It was a rather unusual title for a movie that told a very familiar tale. *I, Monster* was simply the Amicus version of *Dr. Jekyll and Mr. Hyde*, with the names changed. It was far from the best film version of the Robert Louis Stevenson classic, but the use of standing sets on the Shepperton lot gave it an expensive feel, despite the usual limited budget.

For its other 1970 Cushing vehicle, Amicus decided to return to its winning omnibus formula. *The House that Dripped Blood* became a major hit for Amicus, helped by good stories, a seasoned cast, and the inventive framing device of a "House" that tells its tales. Peter appeared in the excellent "Waxworks" segment of the film.

Peter's reunion, of sorts, with a wax Dracula.

At this point in his career, Peter felt quite satisfied with the rewards of his chosen profession, and he made it clear that money was never his main goal anyway.

"I've of course been very lucky," he said. "That's mostly because the public seems to love this type of film. *Curse of Frankenstein* was my first, and that was way back in 1956. I really feel I've been looked after incredibly well. I'm a great believer in having faith. I mean you've got to do your best to insure that things go right, so as not to be a burden upon others. But I feel we are all guided, whether we get what we think is right or not. And whether we get what we think we want in this world isn't actually that important. It's what we are given and what we do with what we are given in this world, that leads us on to the next."

It was at this point in our long discussion that I first became aware of the main reason that this talented actor appeared older and more fragile than I had anticipated. As we wrapped up our discussion of the films Peter did for Amicus in 1970, the actor took me by surprise.

Cushing paused briefly, took a deep breath and said, "You know, I died on January the 14th, 1971, at exactly two minutes past nine in the morning." He quickly explained that he was talking about the loss of his wife Helen. Looking at him as he spoke, it was clear that he had been devastated by her death.

"You know, I owe everything I am in life, what I am as a person and my success in my work ... everything I am and have, she made possible. And strangely enough ... and I hope this doesn't sound egotistical ... I'm a bit shy really as a person. I haven't got a great deal of confidence and I get very self-conscious on a stage. Mind you, I've done a great deal of theater work, but I don't have the attributes that one really needs in the medium. I mean, obviously I was given some degree of talent, and you've got to do the best that you can with that. But you can't say talent is the only thing in life. And it was my beloved Helen who gave me the confidence that I needed."

In a bid to keep himself busy following the loss of his wife, Peter picked up the pace of his film appearances, including his work for Amicus. *Tales from the Crypt* was another anthology film, but this time around the framing device made use of Sir Ralph Richardson in the guise of "The Crypt Keeper." Peter gave a moving performance in the segment entitled "Poetic Justice," playing an elderly man tormented by his neighbors. And he was just as effective disguised as a ghoul seeking revenge from beyond the grave.

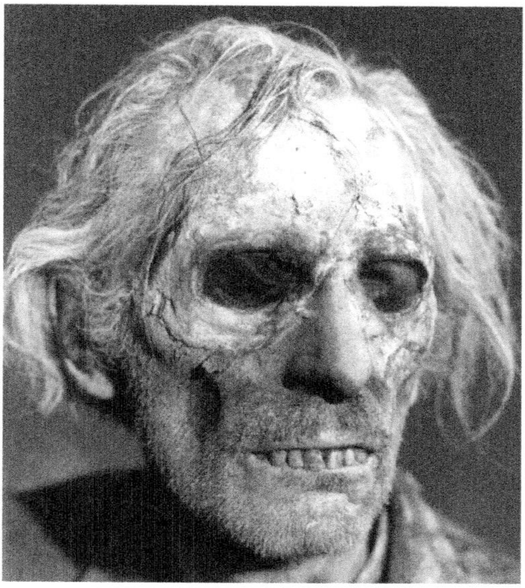

The film was quite successful thanks to the fact that it was based on the EC comic book of the same name, had a number of additional name actors including Joan Collins and Richard Greene, and gave the general impression of high production values.

Asylum (1971) was yet another entry in the Amicus omnibus sweepstakes. The Robert Bloch script for the film was quite good and Peter, as usual, turned in an excellent performance.

Once again, however, Cushing did not play a part in the framing device. In *Asylum* the stories unfold amid a guessing game involving the identity of a mental patient who knows only too well what it feels like to be "An inmate running the asylum."

The next Amicus attempt at an episodic film would, like *Tales from the Crypt*, draw again on EC comics, but Peter Cushing would not be featured in the movie. *Vault of Horror*, which unfortunately lacked the expensive look of many other Amicus offerings, is perhaps best known today for the appearance of an actor who would later play *Dr. Who*,

Tom Baker.

Meanwhile, Glynis Johns, though well past her starlet days, gives a rather sexy portrayal of a deadly wife. And, in a casting surprise, Terry-Thomas plays her husband. It's rather unusual to see the British comedian being featured in an Amicus horror movie, but he does an excellent job playing a man who gets "hammered."

While Cushing is sorely missed in this film, he was about to embark on an ambitious movie schedule that would give the impression that he was virtually everywhere at the same time. In his attempt to remain busy following his wife's death, he committed himself to a string of pictures.

"Just in the one year" (after Helen died,) I don't really remember much about the first four months, but I did a picture around April, and in the following year - from April to April - I did eleven films. I wasn't playing the lead, I assure you, because that would be impossible. I was always playing small parts or guest stars. But I didn't go looking for these parts, they came to me in this time when I was at rock bottom and needed them most. I just think it shows how one is looked after."

One 1972 non-anthology film that presented Peter with a chance to keep busy was the gothic horror *And Now the Screaming Starts* from Amicus. In this period piece, Peter plays a doctor who investigates an ancient curse.

In addition to his work for Amicus, Peter appeared in films for Hammer, Tigon, American-International and even in the Benmar/Granada co-production *Horror Express*

which was shot in Spain and also featured Christopher Lee. It seemed amazing to me that this veteran actor could juggle all of these projects. When Peter and I met in 1973 he was working on two Amicus films at virtually the same time.

While we talked at Twickenham studios, where *Madhouse* was being shot under the direction of Jim Clark, fellow-director Kevin Connor and his crew members were over at Shepperton, still shooting individual stories for Peter's latest omnibus film, *From Beyond the Grave*. He shuttled between the two and shot additional scenes on location at Pyrford Place in Surrey.

From Beyond the Grave was an intelligent film with some excellent stories and featured talented performers like Donald and Angela Pleasence.

As was the case with *Dr. Terror's House of Horrors*, Peter would be the glue holding the tales in *From Beyond the Grave* together. He plays the proprietor of an antiques shop and the film is about the fate of his customers.

Since Peter provides the framing device, Subotsky

arranged to have his scenes shot at the same time to save on cost. But Cushing still had time to add his own special touches. He told me he learned to love the way movies were shot when he first made a few in America.

"That's why I love to do films. They're all done in little pieces. I mean, you've got to know the whole concept of the part overall, but you haven't got an audience until they go to the cinema. By then, you're work is done. And that's why I enjoy this medium above all."

It took quite a while for Peter to return from his early visit to America, mostly because of money problems. Despite the fact that he was homesick almost as soon as he arrived in Hollywood, he managed to persevere. The star of *The Man in the Iron Mask*, Louis Hayward, gave Peter a helping hand.

"Louis Hayward was terribly kind to me. He was married to Ida Lupino at the time, and I went up to their place for a weekend, and wound up staying for a year. So that shows the kind of friends they were, bless them. And, of course, I met nearly every Englishman in Hollywood at the time, including Aubrey Smith, Cary Grant and the great Boris Karloff. I was really just a fan...simply agog!"

But Peter's screen appearances were few and far between at the time, and his desire to return to England was growing, especially with the onset of World War Two.

"People who were in service, like David Niven, were called back immediately," said Cushing. "The rest of us were on standby pending physicals, but I got a low classification because of two accidents I'd had playing rugger, which is rather like your football."

Still, Cushing longed to get back to England. Peter explained:

"When something is wrong at home, you want to be there. There's nothing you can do about it, there's no medicine, nothing you can take. All you want to do is just get home. And homesickness is a very good word for it, because that's just what it is, an illness, a nasty thing."

Unfortunately, it would take Peter quite some time to make his way back to England.

"Even if I had the money, which I certainly didn't, you couldn't just hop on a plane or a boat because most of them were commandeered for the war effort. But eventually I had saved up enough money to get to New York, and I thought that was a step in the right direction. I remember seeing a notice over a hospital that said, 'Give Blood for Britain.' So I thought, 'Here's something I've got that I can give.' And I popped in, gave them a pint, came out and fell flat on my face. They had to give me two pints, so there was my war effort down the drain."

Obviously Peter's health at the time was hardly robust, but he said that was mostly because of his diet.

"At that time, I either worked and ate, or I didn't work and didn't eat. So I was at a very low ebb, but you know what you are like when you're young. You can keep going until something hits you. Well, something hit me and I was in hospital for two weeks. And they said, 'you better go somewhere to get some sun and relax' — you know, all these marvelous things they tell you — and you think, 'fine, just give me a couple of hundred pounds and I will.' But I was again very lucky, and I think it shows how one is watched over and looked after. There's a place up in the Adirondacks called Warrensburg, where there was a summer camp. The director's name was Wilbur Sparrow, and he knew of the work I'd done in Hollywood, which for a lucky beginner, wasn't really bad. I mean I'd done a few pictures of some sort of note. But I had been lucky in a sad sort of way, because most English people were back home for the war. So when there was a call for an Englishman, there were so few around that I was chosen. That was sort of an ill wind blowing nobody any good, but for me it was a touch of luck, though one I wasn't too happy about because of the circumstances. Anyway, I got the job in Warrensburg at this summer camp for holiday makers where they had a different type of entertainment every night. John Ireland was also there, this was before he became well-known, and he and I were great friends. We rehearsed six plays and that was the only hard work, rehearsing the plays. Because, once we got them going, we only played once a week at night and one matinee a week. All the rest of the week we had off, because they had other entertainment. One night they'd have a dancer, then a variety show, then a play. The place was surrounded by lovely lakes and we lived in log cabins, and that was a great recouping place for me. Plus it was near the Canadian border. And we were there for three months and we got all our keep plus a hundred dollars. Well, the hundred dollars went for smokes and jugs of milk and things because they were extras."

Peter would have to continue to scrimp and save after he finished summer camp duty with John Ireland. Ireland, by the way, would one day work at the company that eventually became Hammer. He starred in *The Glass Cage* (aka *The Glass Tomb*,) a 1955 Exclusive Films co-production with the American firm Lippert.)

Peter eventually got down to New York City where he and Ireland stayed at the Y.M.C.A., spending a lot of time, according to Peter, playing Parcheesi!

However, Peter finally got what he thought would be his big break.

"There were two plays offered to me. One was called *R.A.F* and the other was called *The Seventh Trumpet*. Well, I picked *The Seventh Trumpet* because it was a jolly good part of a cockney policeman. It turned out that I chose the right one, because my play ran two weeks and *R.A.F.* only lasted one week. I shall never forget, though, one critic said, *The Seventh Trumpet* opened last night on Broadway and blew its last blast!"

When the money from *Trumpet* ran out, Cushing was broke again. But John Ireland came to the rescue. Peter explained:

"One day John said, 'look, you've done some work in Hollywood, now that you're out of a job you should have some benefits coming.' Well, it was welcome news to me. I had never looked at any benefit deductions they were taking out, I just looked at my pay packet. Well, after I applied for it, I got fifteen dollars a week for several weeks, which really went a long way back then."

Eventually, Peter made his way up to Montreal. He felt making it to Canada would bring him closer to his goal of finding a way back home.

"I kept writing to the head of the British Command in Canada...they were ferrying troops back and forth. And I still have the letters they sent back thanking me for my patriotism but saying they didn't have room. Anyway, I did all sorts of jobs in Canada...I was a theater usher, a night clerk, worked at a car park. Funny enough, there was a film run not too long ago on the telly called *Captain of the Clouds* with James Cagney. The next day someone asked me if I'd ever seen it before and, in true Noel Coward fashion, I said 'Yes, I saw it fifty-seven times!' It was playing in the Montreal movie house where I worked as an usher. And once I was nearly arrested when I was working for a small film studio that produced documentaries. They assigned me to paint some swastikas and Japanese flags, because they needed them on a map that appeared in one of the films. I took my assignment home to the Y.M.C.A. where I was staying at the time. I popped out briefly to get a cup of coffee and when I came back there were a couple of Canadian Mounties there. The sweet Irish cleaning lady had reported me. But I understood. She liked me very much but she thought it was her duty."

Nova Scotia was the next stop for Cushing.

"I finally made my way up to Halifax, where there was a convoy about to head for England. The captain said he was sure there would be a deserter before the ship left that night, and if I showed up I could take his place. He asked me what I could do, and when I told him I was an actor, he seemed to be having second thoughts. But I think he had a soft spot in his heart for the arts so he let me come along. On my first day, I was assigned to the crow's nest. I got up top and started yelling for help. Sad to say, they couldn't actually hear me, but they did realize that I was yelling. Finally, they sent a couple of fellows up to get me down. Then the captain called me to his cabin. He was a very nice fellow and he decided to take me off crow's nest duty."

So, through the good offices of a captain who liked actors, Cushing made it back to Britain, where he soon managed to find a reasonable amount of stage work He was the male lead in the touring version of Noel Coward's *Private Lives*, and also appeared in a West End production of *War and Peace*. But overall, it was a rather lean period for the young actor. Peter told me, however, that he often recalled fondly those days following his return to Britain from America.

"They were the most wonderful times because I married my wife after I got back to England. Financially, it was a rough time, but of course I look back on it now with great love and great nostalgia."

As Peter and I continued to talk, I thought back to earlier

in the day when Peter was shooting a scene with Vincent Price. These two were such professionals. Peter told me the acting bug bit him early.

"I think really before I knew anything about acting, I was always playing 'Let's Pretend.' It's really always been with me. I was really never any good at anything else."

Ranking high on the list of reasons for the success that Amicus enjoyed was its use of the same talented personnel both in front of and behind the camera. Peter, of course, was a prime example when it came to actors Amicus sought to use on a regular basis. But there were writers, directors and technical folks that Amicus used over and over again in film after film too. As far as writing was concerned, if Milt Subotsky wasn't doing the stories and screenplays himself, he would usually use famed *Psycho* author Robert Bloch. Meanwhile, helping to give its films a more expensive look were talented art directors like Tony Curtis (no relation to the actor of the same name) and Don Mingaye. And Freddie Francis and Roy Ward Baker were among the company's favorite directors.

Freddie Francis

Many of these talented people also worked their magic at Hammer. There too, said Cushing, working with a crew of regulars was important.

"They always stuck to the same team of people, not just actors like Christopher (Lee) and myself, but the same directors, the same musical conductors and so on. I think one of the yardsticks of Hammer's success was that they were tremendous people. Now, when we first started at Bray, it was a very confined studio. It was actually an old house that they had bought, and when we needed a bedroom set we went up to the bedroom, where there was a four-poster bed, and we shot in the bedroom. On the proceeds of the first Frankenstein film, they built a very small sound stage. And gradually, over the years, they built it into such a wonderfully compact lot that we had three or four sound stages."

Peter wouldn't make his last film for Amicus until 1976, when he appeared in *At the Earth's Core,* a sci-fi/adventure/comedy aimed primarily at children. But his last *horror* film for the company was *The Beast Must Die,* (1973) in which he played a werewolf expert.

Amicus shot quickly, rarely resorting to more than a few takes on any one scene. Cushing's years in television helped prepare him for this approach. It was pretty hectic behind-the-scenes for people like Peter back then. He was one of the busiest actors in early British TV and got a crash course in working fast. While the experience served him well later at Amicus and Hammer, he said it was hard work:

"Of course, I learned a great deal about everything during those years. Things weren't easy, I must admit, for a number of years. You see, when I started in television it was all live. You needed as much rehearsal time for that one performance as you did for the theater. You would rehearse for at least 3 weeks, then go on live on a Sunday and repeat the live performance on Thursday. Looking back on it, it's a wonder that I'm not a nervous wreck today, because it really was most nerve-racking. And for those five weeks of work on each television play, I would receive the princely sum of thirty pounds. Of course, the pay did get better later on, but not all that much better. So I went out of one television performance into the next, just to get enough money to live."

Working under those conditions, Peter became a very quick study. As word of his talent spread within the early TV industry, he wound up getting more and more television work.

But that was a double-edged sword. On the plus side, he was becoming well known among TV fans. On the minus side, back in those days the very fact that an actor's name was associated with television could be enough to keep the major movie studios from hiring you.

It was Peter who reminded me of this and who told me that, in a roundabout way, it's what led him to Hammer.

"I did solid television in England for several years and became frightfully well-known on British TV screens. And at that time cinema was really feeling the pinch of television. Now they're getting into sort of a marriage, but then they weren't even looking at each other ... sort of arch-enemies. Then nobody in movies wanted to have anything to do with anyone in television. Only one company was interested in television, and that was Hammer. They had already been taking radio programs and turning them into spin-off films."

Dick Barton was among the radio characters brought to the screen by Hammer and distributed by Exclusive. The company made three films in all: *Dick Barton: Special Agent*, *Dick Barton at Bay*, and *Dick Barton Strikes Back.*

Peter went on to explain that, because the people at Hammer were already quite familiar with his work and weren't prejudiced against TV actors, they approached him early on:

"Well, all the plays I had been doing on television weren't new. They were old established parts and you really only had to be half-good to go over well in them because they were all splendid. So Hammer was familiar with my work and they wanted me to do things for them. The people at Hammer got in touch with my agent, but I couldn't accept because I was under contract to do these television programs. Then, when my three years with the B.B.C. were up, I read in the trade papers that Hammer was to make a color version of *Frankenstein,* which I'd seen with Boris Karloff and Colin Clive years before. I felt if it was anything like the original, I'd want to be in it. And that's how it all started, without any idea in anyone's mind that this incredible snowball would start."

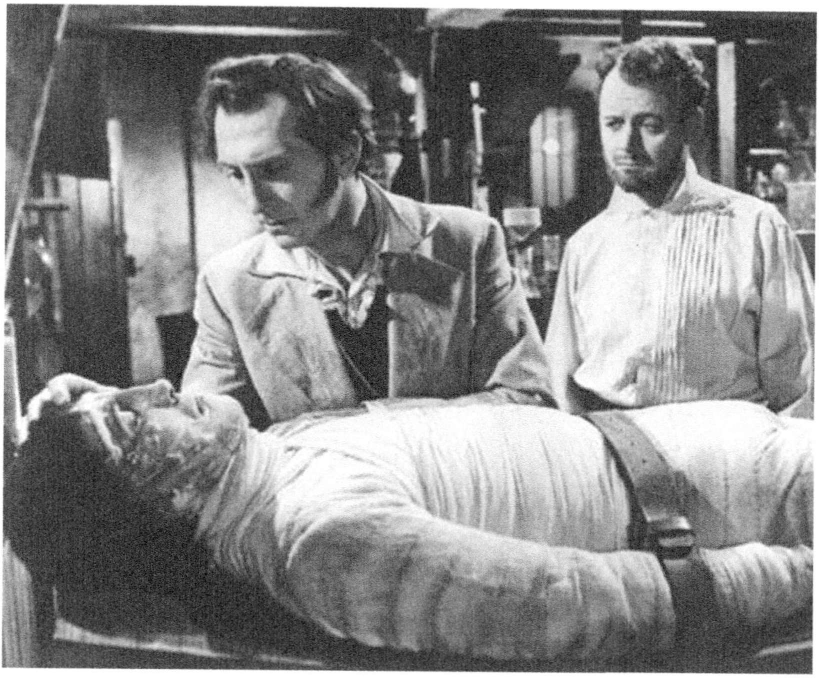

Peter said the snowball effect began as soon as Hammer saw the box office returns for the movie.

"The film was, of course, a tremendous success, and ... in all industries ... it's extremely important to make money. If a picture makes money you make more like it. If not, you're out of business. So the success of this film insured that there would be others. And that was way back in 1956."

Cushing paused, as if to consider the length of time since making *The Curse of Frankenstein.* He seemed genuinely surprised that it had been 17 years prior to our discussion. We were both kidding around at that point, and I said "Ah, but you don't look a day older." Without missing a beat Peter responded, "Thank you dear boy, but you'll notice I have quite a bit of hair pasted on my head!" This was typical of

Cushing. He was always modest to an extreme. His comment earlier about the quality of the material making him look good on TV was an exaggeration too. Cushing's talent is what made him look good and it explains why Hammer wanted him.

It was the little of pieces of "business" that Peter added to all his roles that made his appearances so special. It was obvious in his earliest Amicus film, *Doctor Terror's House of Horrors,* and carried through to the ones he was shooting and preparing to shoot when I was there. In *Dr. Terror* you can see it in the way Peter caresses the tarot cards, turning them over in hands covered with fingerless gloves. It's also evident in the looks he gives a skeptical Christopher Lee, and the way he flips through the cards before calling the deck his *House of Horrors.* It was the same in later films such as *And Now the Screaming Starts* and *The Beast Must Die.* In these and other films his roles called for mannerisms not unlike those he displayed in his several appearances as Sherlock Holmes.

"Whenever I'm offered anything, if I know there's a book ... that it was taken from a book ... I always read it because I feel the author must know the character he created. There are so many Sherlock Holmes stories which I read originally when I was a boy, and I went through all of them again. And in every one of those books, I found a facet of his character. I mean Holmes had so many quirks, like keeping his bills under a jack-knife on the mantelpiece, the violin, treating Watson as a sort of whipping boy, holding his fingertips together and so on."

Even in his roles at Amicus, where the actor sometimes made only brief appearances, he said preparation was the key.

"There's a great deal of work before the actual filming," said Cushing. "You've got to study the part, learn the character and so on. It's not the actual shooting, but the buildup."

Everyone I spoke with behind-the-scenes at Amicus agreed that it was this devotion to his craft that made Peter Cushing's performances so special. He was always prepared, always willing to improvise if a scene needed something extra, always available to less experienced actors who needed a helping hand. Peter had been generous enough to spend a great deal of his time chatting with me and, before we parted, I asked him about his plans for the future.

"My ambition," he said, "is to go on entertaining people ... being the means by which they are entertained ... and in that, I've been very lucky."

And Peter continued to entertain audiences everywhere. Later in his career, he became famous among a whole new generation of fans playing Grand Moff Tarkin in the *Star Wars* saga.

Peter Cushing passed away in August of 1994. My wife and I were extremely saddened by the news, but comforted by the feeling that he was at last reunited with his beloved wife Helen. We both remember this special man fondly.

CHRISTOPHER LEE AT AMICUS

Christopher Lee was the first major horror star to appear in an Amicus film. He was also the first to stop appearing in films for the studio. But there's no doubt that each of the movies in which he was featured benefited greatly from his presence.

Looking back now it's clear that there was a definite time when Lee and Amicus had a parting of the ways. But for those of us who were around at the time, it wasn't so clear cut. Remember, I first met Milton Subotsky only about a year after he had shot *I, Monster* with Lee. And, just prior to that, the two had collaborated on *The House that Dripped Blood*. When the actor didn't show up in *Tales from the Crypt*, I assumed it was just a logistical problem. *Asylum* was in post-production at the time, and when Subotsky's chauffeur told me Peter Cushing was in the movie, I took it for granted that Lee was too.

But by the time I came back to London the following year, I knew that wasn't the case. Not only had Lee's name been absent from the *Asylum* cast credits, but the actor was missing from *And Now the Screaming Starts* as well.

Perhaps I could have even convinced myself that his exclusion from *Vault of Horror* was just a fluke, since even Peter Cushing was absent from that one. However, I was on the set by the time *From Beyond the Grave* was shooting, and when I saw no sign of Lee on that production, I knew the Amicus/Lee relationship was over. What I wanted to know was, why? I would eventually put that question to Milton Subotsky.

But I'm getting ahead of myself. Before we take a look at the end of the relationship, we should, at least briefly, discuss the beginning. Lee's successful collaborations with the studio began with the first Amicus horror film ever, the classic *City of the Dead* discussed in detail elsewhere in this book. It would be hard to imagine the movie with any other actor in the dual roles Lee plays ... projecting confident authority as the professor and personifying evil as the leader of the coven of witches.

At the time Lee was hired for *City of the Dead*, Max Rosenberg and Milton Subotsky knew that he would be a major draw for horror fans, since the actor had already scored in classics like *Curse of Frankenstein, Horror of Dracula* and *The Mummy*. These films had made him famous on both sides of the Atlantic.

Ironically though, leading lady Stevenson wasn't aware of his genre fame. In her intro for the restored VCI Entertainment DVD of the film, she said she just knew him as a talented actor with a great voice, and only learned that she'd been playing opposite a major horror star when she told friends about the film later, and they were so impressed!

Christopher Lee's initial association with Milt Subotsky would be advantageous for both the actor and the producer. Lee was looking to branch out beyond Hammer and to take advantage of his new found star status to make some money at other studios. Lee had received a grand total of £500 from Hammer for *Curse of Frankenstein* and £750 pounds for *Horror of Dracula*.

City of Fear offered Lee the opportunity for a decent pay day, even though the overall budget for the film was low. That's because most of the key personnel on the movie were more than happy to do it, whatever the salary. Scriptwriter George Baxt was a New Yorker brought over by *Robin Hood* producer Hannah Weinstein to work on one of her other television programs. *City of the Dead* would give him his first movie credit, so he had good reason to want the job. The same holds true for John Moxie. It was also his first movie credit as director. Betta St. John's salary was probably quite reasonable, too. At this point she was doing mostly television, including Hanna Weinstein's *Four Just Men*. Venetia Stevenson wasn't a huge name, but she had done a few movies and several television shows in the states before going back to England. She was a lovely addition to the cast, but again, it isn't likely that she cost the producers a great deal.

That should have left a fairly substantial amount of money in the kitty for Lee. However, even if he got the lion's share of the casting budget, it must have still been a bargain for Subotsky, since the budget for the entire film was only £45,000!

While screenwriter George Baxt remembered Lee working only one day on this first horror effort for Milton Subotsky and Max Rosenberg, this would seem highly unlikely due to the amount of screen time he has in the movie. He appears not only in the college scenes, but in the coven scenes in "Whitewood" as well, where ... as Lee put it ... "I was burned to death in a monk's robe!"

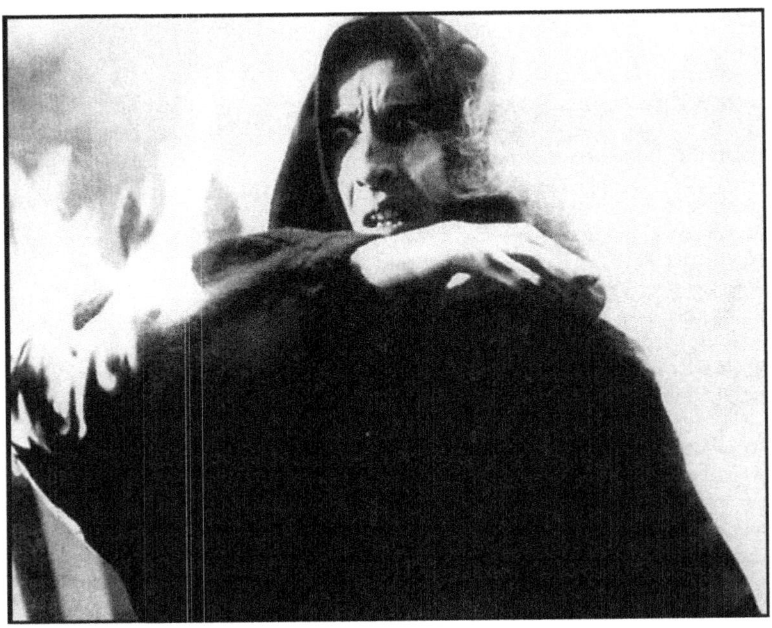

Actually all the viewer sees is the robe catching fire on Lee's arm, but that would have taken some time to rehearse before being filmed. Moreover, Venetia Stevenson indicates she was the first to wrap up her part in the production because scenes were shot in sequence and she dies first. If that's correct, Lee would have had to have been there longer.

In any event, Lee felt good about the way this production was handled and was pleased with the way the film turned out. The actor got a chance to stretch a bit. Lee had a fairly normal role in the beginning of the movie ... not a horrible monster, a vampire with fangs, but a typical ... if rather ill-tempered ... professor.

Lee's experience on *City of the Dead* influenced his decision to agree to appear in *Dr. Terror's House of Horrors* when he was approached by Subotsky a few years later.

Soon, the actor would begin a concerted effort to increase his reputation in Europe as well as in Britain. Lee had the foresight to realize that one day the motion picture industry would be largely a global enterprise relying on international stars. With that in mind, he set about planning his career carefully.

Looking to develop an international reputation and get out from under heavy British taxation, Lee decided a move was in order in 1962. The actor felt Switzerland was the perfect central location for what he hoped would be more work in continental films. As it turned out though, most of the offers were coming from Italy, and work restrictions due to his stay in Switzerland were limiting his British film appearances. The actor was looking to increase his screen visibility, and in 1964 he began work on his first film under the official auspices of Amicus Productions.

By that time, Lee had appeared in a great many movies, some quite good and some quite bad. It's hard to believe that he wasn't tempted, at least some of the time, to walk through them. But that was definitely not the case with the movies he made for Amicus. When he made his first film for Milton Subotsky, Lee was already looking to take a breather from playing monsters at Hammer. He had made *The Curse of Frankenstein, The Horror of Dracula* and *The Mummy* in rapid succession. The *City of the Dead* may have been a horror movie, but it wasn't a monster movie. Lee at least got a chance to play a college professor, albeit one who heads a cult of Satan worshippers on the side. He may be a tad too fanatic about the topic of witchcraft as the professor, but he's perfect as the cult leader.

Five years after Christopher Lee worked for Milton Subotsky and Max Rosenberg in *City of the Dead,* he signed on to appear in *Dr. Terror's House of Horrors.* The first film had officially been attributed to Vulcan Productions, but by now Milt and Max had set up Amicus. The movie proved to be a milestone, paving the way for later Amicus anthology films that would become the Amicus trademark. In *Dr. Terror,* Lee was reunited with Peter Cushing and Donald Sutherland, although they only appeared together in the framing story. Lee had been impressed by Sutherland when he first worked with the young actor in Italy on *The Castle of the Living Dead*. Michael Gough is another familiar face. He appeared in Lee's first Hammer vampire outing, *Horror of Dracula*. They're both perfect for their *Dr. Terror* roles.

Lee plays an arrogant art critic who enjoys mocking a painter played by Gough. But Gough turns the tables on Christopher by finding a way to completely humiliate him. Lee takes revenge by running over Gough, who loses his right hand.

Gough, realizing he will never paint again, kills himself. Ah, but his disembodied hand returns to taunt Lee, and the actor's emotions come full circle ... from pride and self-assurance to humiliation, anger and finally panicky fear. Lee gives a top-rate performance in the film.

Perhaps Rosenberg and Subotsky wrote-off the cost of the articulated hand over a period of years, because Amicus made sure it got more use out of the thing. The bloody stump was still crawling along the floor following Stephanie

Beacham around in *And Now the Screaming Starts.* The disembodied hand showed up in other Amicus productions too, including *Scream and Scream Again.* I sometimes think that if Milton and Max decided to remake *Gone with the Wind,* the Amicus disembodied hand would be clomping along behind Rhett Butler as he carried Scarlett O'Hara down the staircase at the end of the film!

Dr. Terror was quite successful, and Lee soon returned to Amicus to shoot a non-anthology film, *The Skull.* This time his role wasn't all that large and the main purpose he serves in the film is to deliver a warning to Peter Cushing about the dangers of the title artifact.

By this time Freddie Francis was bothered by what he viewed as interference from Milt Subotsky in the editing room. Francis said in his autobiography that he deliberately shot a billiard room sequence in one long take so Milt *couldn't* edit it!

Since Subotsky didn't want to spend any more than £110,000 on *The Skull,* salaries must have been fairly low. Lee often said that he would like to see some of the movies he was making have longer shooting schedules and bigger budgets. However, in many cases, the money just wasn't there.

If the actor had felt his screen time in *The Skull* was limited, as I mentioned earlier, he didn't fare any better in his next Amicus venture, *Scream and Scream Again.* Like *The Skull* this was another non-anthology film which normally would have provided a larger role. But American International was co-producing and Deke Heyward was mainly interested in squeezing Vincent Price, Lee and Cushing into the same picture for marquee value. Lee is often just pictured in his office giving dictation or speaking on the phone.

The director was Gordon Hessler, with whom both Lee and Price had worked the previous year on *The Oblong Box.*

It's a shame Christopher Lee and Vincent Price didn't get to appear together more often, or to at least share more screen time in those films in which they did appear. In *The Oblong Box* Lee's part is just a cameo. He and Price have only one scene together, but they had fun with it. Lee told my childhood pal Bill Kelley, who grew up to become friends with the actor, that Price ... wearing a huge cape ... comes upon Lee who lies dying on the floor, and is supposed to bend down and roll him over. Unfortunately, Price rolled Lee onto his cape, and had trouble getting back up. Neither one of them could stop laughing.

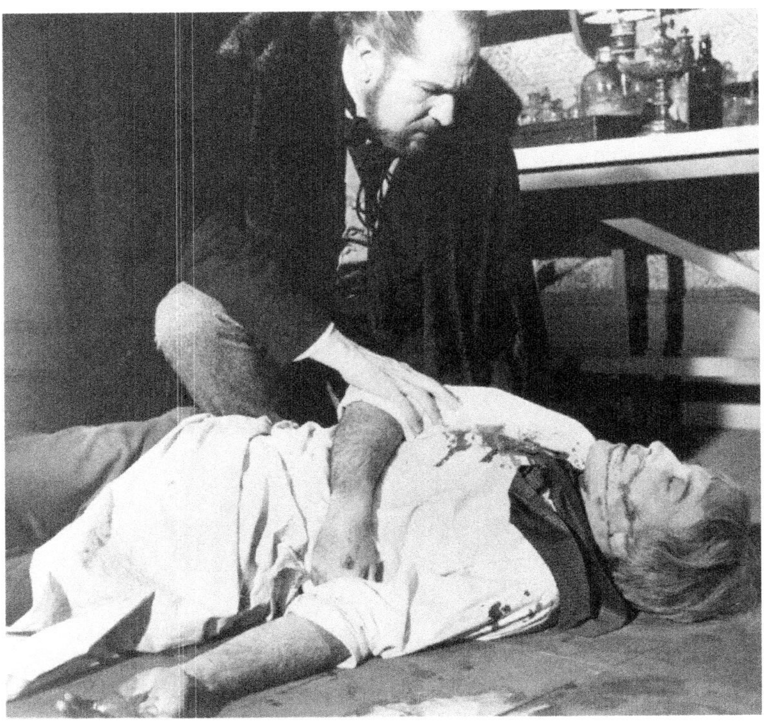

It wasn't an isolated instance. A good sense of humor was something Price and Lee shared. The one thing Lee was serious about, however, was his career. He had been back in England for several years now, and was keeping himself busy. But the movies he was making were hardly helping in his campaign for international stardom. The actor's love/hate relationship with Hammer continued, as the studio kept pressuring him to do more Dracula movies. Lee made several other films as well, and also found time for two more Amicus outings.

The first of these was the best since *Dr. Terror's House of Horrors*. Called *The House That Dripped Blood*, thanks to Max Rosenberg's imaginative way with a title, the omnibus film gave Lee a chance to put his acting chops on display. Lee's character has to deal with an evil young daughter. have mysterious powers. Actors are always urged never to share screen time with children or dogs, but in the "Sweets to the Sweet" section of the film, Lee manages to hold his own. The actor is just right for the strict father. If you re-watch the segment with the end in mind, you'll recognize the ways he keeps the viewer guessing. For example, Lee greedily grabs a doll from his sweet young daughter, and only later do we learn she would have used it for witchcraft.

It was Lee who reportedly came up with the idea of having the character played by Jon Pertwee in "The Cloak" segment of *The House That Dripped Blood,* be a horror movie star. Robert Bloch's original story was simply about a man who wore a vampire cape to a masquerade party.

Apparently the Pertwee part was planned for Lee, but he wound up playing in "Sweets to the Sweet" instead. As it turned out, the future "Dr. Who" added a perfect comedic touch to the role.

Lee's final appearance in an Amicus film was in *I, Monster* which began shooting in the fall of 1970. Lee had high hopes for this re-telling of the Jekyll and Hyde story and he was pleased with his performance in the movie. However, he was frustrated by the technical problems that developed when Subotsky originally attempted to shoot the film in a 3-D process that necessitated constant camera movement.

While Lee was quite positive about *Dr. Terror's House of Horrors* and *The House that Dripped Blood*, he felt the camera movement in *I, Monster* made the movie more difficult to edit and took away from the film. Lee was also unhappy with the title Subotsky had chosen. He couldn't understand why anyone would use *I, Monster* for a movie that was essentially another screen version of Jekyll and Hyde.

Lee of course was right. It was the story of Jekyll and Hyde and Subotsky simply switched the names to Dr. Marlow and Mr. Blake. But there was a method to Milton's madness. He felt a movie with the character-name and title changes would help attract a bigger audience than one billed as yet another Jekyll/Hyde remake.

After *I, Monster* wrapped, an 11-year relationship came to an end. Christopher Lee would never make another film for the team of Milton Subotsky and Max Rosenberg. While future Amicus productions would continue to feature Peter Cushing, Lee would be among the missing. It's a shame because, in many ways, Lee's performances in the Amicus films were far better than ones he gave in some of his best-known Hammer movies.

For example, Lee was at a distinct disadvantage in some of the later Dracula roles he wound up playing. Hammer would pre-sell Dracula films to distributors by indicating that Lee would star. Only later would the studio approach Lee, who had no intention of appearing in another Dracula. Sometimes Hammer would re-work the script to cut out Lee's part, be forced by distributors to put Lee back in, finally get Lee to agree, and realize they were stuck with a script that gave Lee little to do in the finished film. It was a real mess and wasn't fair to the actor or to Hammer fans. Amicus, on the other hand, always provided the actor with solid roles, even in the omnibus films.

It's fascinating to speculate on the effects a continuation of Lee's association with Amicus would have had on the studio's remaining genre films. Would Lee have once again donned his *City of the Dead* monk-like robe to play the Crypt Keeper in *Tales from the Crypt*? Or would he have appeared in one of the *Tales from the Crypt* stories, perhaps taking the role that went to Nigel Patrick as the heartless head of a home for the blind?

In *Asylum*, it's tantalizing to imagine Lee playing Dr. Rutherford who greets Robert Powell when he arrives at Dunsmore. Or perhaps the actor would have appeared as Dr. Byron, the patient played by Herbert Lom who was so fascinated by little dolls.

As for Amicus' excursion into gothic horror, *And Now the Screaming Starts*, the part of the evil Henry Fengriffen, which was also played by Lom, would seem tailor-made for

Lee. And, in the next film from Subotsky and Rosenberg, *Vault of Horror*, maybe Christopher could have been persuaded to take the Curt Jurgens role, playing the greedy magician who would stop at nothing to add to his bag of tricks. Lee would have added a whole new dimension to the part. Jurgens came off as just another con artist, while Lee would have almost certainly brought a degree of sophistication to the role.

It's also easy to imagine Lee in the follow-up to *Vault*, *From Beyond the Grave*. He would have been perfect for the role of the man who cheats Peter Cushing on an antique mirror, only to get it home and learn that it's haunted.

And, suppose Lee was in the cast of *Madhouse*? It would have been easy for him to slip into Robert Quarry's role as Oliver Quayle, the sleazy producer pictured with Adrienne Corri below.

Even better, what if Price took the Quarry role .... nobody plays "sleazy" like Vincent ... and Lee took the lead? It would have been an entirely different picture. For one thing, the character of *Dr. Death* would probably be changed to a horror movie vampire, and the clips would come from Lee's old Hammer films. Now *that* would be something to see!

The actor also would have had several possible choices if he decided to appear in *The Beast Must Die*. He could have played Calvin Lockhart's role, as the millionaire determined to catch a werewolf. Or he could have replaced Anton Diffring as the man who oversees security on the estate and doesn't believe in werewolves until it's too late. Unfortunately, though, it's doubtful that even the presence of Lee would improve this final Amicus horror film all that much.

But speculating about what would have happened had Christopher Lee continued working for Amicus is, of course, an exercise in frustration. The fact is he didn't. And the question is, why? Subotsky was quite direct with me when I asked the question. From his point of view, it was a matter of money. Lee's asking price had gone up and Subotsky didn't feel he could afford him anymore. He told me he had spoken with Lee's agent but hadn't really had any luck. Because Amicus and Lee had history together, I think Subotsky thought the agent might be willing to give the studio a break, but it didn't happen.

Another reason Milton felt Lee might be inclined to continue with Amicus was the relative high quality of the company's films. At this point, Lee's name was being associated with some real stinkers. The number of alternate titles a film has is usually a bad sign. And the movie known as *Philosophy in the Boudoir/Eugenie—The Story of Her Journey into Perversion/De Sade '70*, was bad indeed. Bill Kelley told me that Lee complained some distasteful sex scenes were added to the movie after he completed his work. That may be true, but the public had no way of knowing that at the time and films like this did little for the actor's reputation.

Milton felt Lee would be much better off accepting a bit less money and appearing in quality films. From Subotsky's point of view, meeting the demands of Lee's agent simply wasn't possible if Amicus was to maintain that quality. Milton never discussed Lee's asking price with me. It wouldn't have been like him to do so. But the money allotted for the entire cast on some Amicus productions was less than £20,000. Considering the number of "Names" in these films, paying a few thousand to each star would make sense...some a little more, some a little less. But if any one actor got a whole lot more it would eat up too much of the casting budget.

So money was one reason that Lee's association with

Amicus ended. Subotsky told me he simply felt Lee had priced himself out of Amicus' reach. I don't think there were hard feelings on either side. Although some have pointed to Lee's frustration while shooting *I, Monster* as a possible reason for ending his association, I doubt that was really the case. It's true that the actor wasn't happy with the technical problems caused by the original attempt to film in 3-D. But, in the end, Lee was pleased with his performance. The big problem was that Amicus wasn't providing the types of roles that he now needed to reach his career goals. Remember, Lee was determined to become an international star. For that he needed larger roles in major movies. But, after *I, Monster* four of the next five horror movies Amicus was planning were anthology films, beginning with *Tales from the Crypt.*

Ian Hendry in *Tales from the Crypt*

In his autobiography, Lee was quite direct about his thoughts at the time with regard to any additional anthologies.

"A role in a portmanteau film of four stories was no way to keep a name before the public."

So the actor had no real desire to make a career out of these types of pictures. He had guessed correctly that the era of global production on a massive scale would soon begin, and he wanted to get larger roles that would pave the way for the world-wide stardom he eventually achieved.

But that didn't mean Lee wouldn't work with Milt again if the right vehicle came along. In a 1984 interview with Lawrence French, later published by *Cinefantastique* magazine, Lee told of getting a message from his agent asking whether he'd like to do another film with Milton Subotsky. Lee responded, "Yes, after all these years, what does he have planned?" But the title, *The Monster Club,* proved to be a turnoff for the actor.

Price, Carradine, wolfman in *The Monster Club*

Lee apparently would have preferred something more serious, like the Amicus films he had worked on years before. And considering the reception *The Monster Club* initially received, it looks like Lee made the right decision. The point is, he actually seemed enthusiastic about getting together with Milton again.

So, in the end, the parting of the ways between Lee and Amicus wasn't part of any complicated, dramatic plan. Instead, it all came down to what could be called dollars and sense. Milton Subotsky and Christopher Lee couldn't agree on *dollars*, and Lee had the *sense* to know that it was time to expand his career by concentrating on bigger parts in bigger pictures. Christopher Lee passed away in June of 2015. However, it's nice to remember that, for one brief period in time, the combination of the words "Amicus Productions" and "Christopher Lee" meant movie magic!

VINCENT PRICE AT AMICUS

Vincent Price said he'd join us for lunch as soon as he got some of his makeup off. Novelist Angus Hall was already in the canteen at Twickenham Studios, where Price and Peter Cushing were filming the screen version of Hall's latest book.

Price joined us at a table at the far end of the commissary about 20 minutes later, and my wife would join us shortly after that. Vincent's face was supposed to be horribly burned in the previous shot, which he had to finish up after lunch. So the makeup department left half of the gooey mess on. That way, he could eat through one side of his mouth and there'd be less makeup to apply after lunch.

Price in full makeup for *Madhouse*.

It was a little weird to see Price with half of his face appearing normal and the other half looking like melted pizza. When my wife Pat joined us, the actor's "bad side" was facing the window. I had gotten used to the way he looked by this time, so I really thought nothing about it. But before I could say anything, Vincent got up and faced my wife as, ever the gentleman he pulled out a chair for her. My wife jumped a mile! Luckily for me, she has a great sense of humor ... more than 45 years later we're still married!

Vincent Price was a Hollywood professional, and he was always willing to go out of his way to help promote his movies. This, of course, made him extremely popular with most producers. But it was both a blessing and a curse for fans. The good news was, there would always be plenty of material available on Vincent Price in newspapers and magazines when he was appearing in an upcoming movie. It was the same if he was plugging a book or some art project for Sears Roebuck.

The bad news for fans was that these types of articles were usually done by any warm body that was available at the newspaper or magazine when the public relations person set up the interview. This often meant the person asking the questions knew little about Price, other than the fact that he was a movie star, and even less about horror films. The catch 22 in all of this was that interviewers who were more likely to obtain the types of information fans would like to learn were less likely to get an interview.

All those years ago, as I made my way across a British soundstage to ask Vincent Price if he could take time out to talk with me, I wasn't at all sure of the response I'd get. First, I was only in my early twenties, so I probably looked like some kid who was asking for an interview for the school paper. And second, Price had just finished a rough morning of shooting. So, understandably, he was polite but not overly enthusiastic when I asked if he might have time for an interview. (I had actually spoken with Price once before, back in the States but that was by phone, so he had no idea what I looked like.) The fact is, I think he was trying to come up with an excuse to get rid of me when, sensing this was not going well, I hastily mentioned that American International had helped set up my visit and that Amicus had suggested the interview. Next, I reached into my bag for the tape recorder I always carried, which had the logos of several well-known news organizations on it. (I may have been young, but I had been free-lancing from the time I was in college.)

This brought about a miraculous transformation. Suddenly, the actor was more than gracious and came up with a simple plan. He suggested that I tag along with him to the makeup department and we could do some of our talking on the way. Then we could meet for lunch and continue the discussion.

I was certainly grateful for the actor's sudden willingness to spare some time for me and I've thought about it often over the years. It was the first time I noticed the major difference between certain types of celebrities. A Hollywood personality like Vincent Price had many demands on his time and he chose to concentrate on those people and things that he thought were most important to his career. When he did, he could be very gracious. Price was a professional at getting along with the people he felt it necessary to cultivate. And that persona served the actor very well throughout his career.

On the other hand, I couldn't help but compare Price to Peter Cushing. I got the impression Peter could care less about where I came from, whether I was important or if I had some connection to the production company. And this may sound like a small thing, but what I remember most about Peter was how he went out of his way to include my wife in all of our conversations. My wife really loved him.

And it was very clear that he simply enjoyed speaking with people ... especially people who had followed his career closely and really enjoyed listening to him.

Don't get me wrong, Vincent Price was very friendly but his was more of a professional friendliness. He certainly came through on his promise to let me follow him to the makeup department. We left the sound stage, made our way through racks of costumes in the wardrobe section, and finally wound up just outside the room where the ugly goo on Vincent's face would be removed. Well, actually, only half of it would be removed...enough so that he could eat comfortably and my wife could, as mentioned earlier, be scared out of her wits.

But as we sat there talking before I headed up to the canteen, I began to realize that, in one way, Vincent Price and Milton Subotsky were a lot alike. Neither one felt the films for which they were most famous could be pigeonholed into the "horror" genre. Milton thought of them as "adult fairy tales," and Vincent surprised me when we talked about which of his many films he viewed as his first horror movie.

Even though Price appeared with Boris Karloff and Basil Rathbone in 1939's *Tower of London,* I thought that might fall into the historical drama category, so I nominated the following year's *The Invisible Man Returns.*

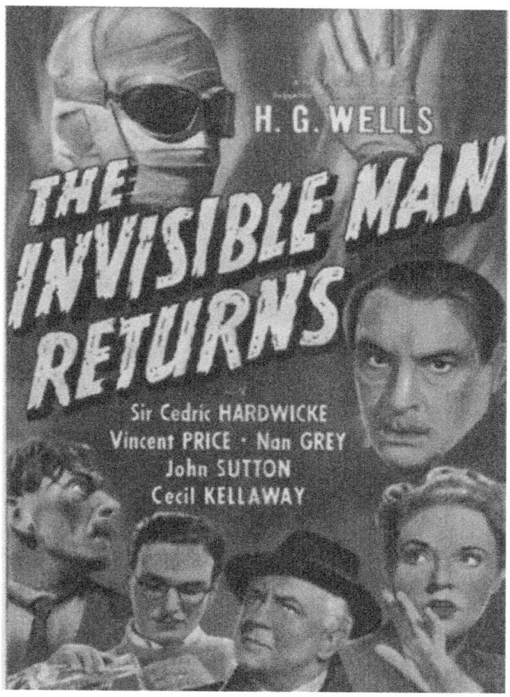

"Oh no," he said. "I think of *The Invisible Man Returns* as science fiction. It was just a logical follow-up to the original with Claude Rains. It certainly wasn't a gothic tale." Then Price laughed and added, "When I was over at Universal (years later) they had me dub the voice of the Invisible Man for *Abbott and Costello Meet Frankenstein,* and that definitely wasn't a real horror film." Price was just a brief invisible presence at the end of the movie, but fans immediately knew his unique voice.

It was in *The Invisible Man Returns* that Vincent's voice would first be used to greatest advantage. For the most part the actor's face is "under wraps" and his voice is the only real means to display emotion.

Co-star Nan Grey with Price.

The Invisible Man Returns was successful and Price, with his dulcet tones, proved a worthy successor to Claude Rains. Indeed the actor's voice could be said to account for almost his entire performance in *The Invisible Man Returns*, where his face is seen only briefly, when he materializes at the end.

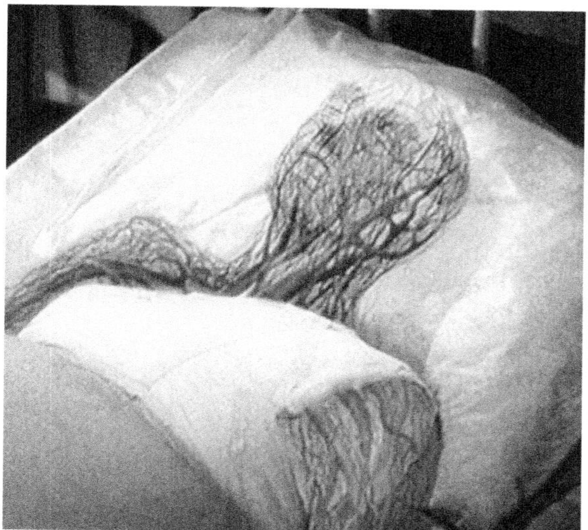

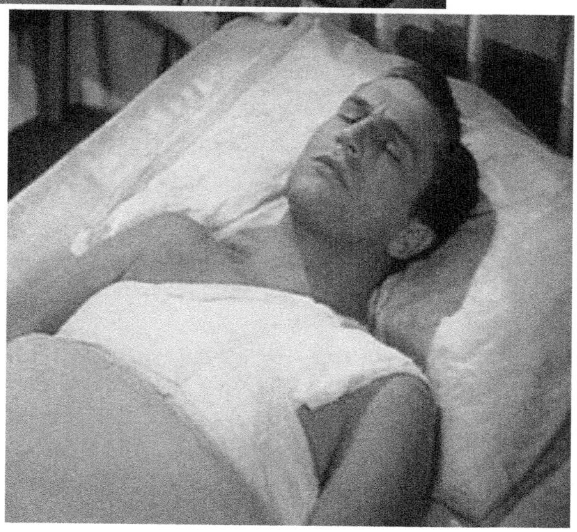

And, despite what Price said to be me about the science fiction aspects of the film, it certainly contained many of Universal's horror flourishes as well. The fog-bound sets, the lab experiments, Price going gradually mad, Sir Cedric Hardwicke scared out of his wits ... all of these touches add to the fear factor in the movie. In addition to Hardwicke, who co-starred with Karloff in 1933's *The Ghoul* and who soon would be featured in *The Ghost of Frankenstein*, Price was surrounded by a "Who's Who" of horror. Cecil Kellaway would show up in *The Mummy's Hand* that same year and would later co-star in *The Beast from 20,000 Fathoms*. Forrester Harvey appeared in the original version of *The Invisible Man* and would soon pop up in *The Wolf Man*. And Harry Cording, who would also have a small role in *The Wolf Man*, appeared in most of Universal's *Sherlock Holmes* series and earlier Universal horrors like *The Black Cat* with Boris Karloff and Bela Lugosi.

Some 32 years after making *The Invisible Man Returns*, Price told me he was well aware that his distinctive vocal style had been a major asset in this film. He said it served him well throughout his entire movie career, especially in the horror genre for which he later became famous:

"A good voice and on screen presence are really important to playing these roles," said Price. "That certainly helped me over the years. It was the same case with Boris Karloff, who was always a good friend of mine."

After the brief contract Price had with Universal expired, he was picked up by Fox, where he made some of his best films, including 1944's *Laura* with Gene Tierney and Dana Andrews. In 1946 Price was again teamed with Tierney in the Fox film *Dragonwyck*.

But by 1947, his contract with Fox was coming to an end. So, Price set his sights on freelancing. He soon got involved with the new medium of television as well as films. But his career seemed to lack direction and it wasn't until 1953 that a turning point would come. Price appeared in the 3-D remake of Warner's 1933 *Mystery of the Wax Museum*. Now entitled *House of Wax*, it was a hit.

Price said *House of Wax* was the film that really marked

him as a horror star and changed his life forever. And, make no mistake about it, at the time Price felt it was a good change. He was in his forties when the role came along, a time when leading-man roles become more difficult to find. The actor told me the screen personality he developed for the movie helped assure him of film stardom ... *and* a healthy income ... for the rest of his career.

He was quite modest about the success of *House of Wax*, though, saying the fact that the 3-D craze was at its height had a lot to do with the film's popularity. But Price himself has to get credit as well. He was perfect, both as his usual suave self and as a disfigured monster.

This role paved the way for the character he would play in so many films to come, right up to and including the role he was playing at Twickenham Studios where we were discussing his career. Ironically in that film, *Madhouse*, Price plays a character who is injured in a fire and wears an outfit very similar to the one in *House of Wax*, complete with cape and slouch hat.

Madhouse hit closer to home than most of Vincent's movies because he was playing an aging horror film star. And so, in our real-life conversation a question arose about the reel-life topic of the film. I asked Vincent whether it bothered him that, from a certain point on in his career, he was almost always playing the villain:

"No not at all. The heavy or character part is usually the best part in the picture and has a lot more facets to it than the part of the hero. The hero role is pretty straightforward from beginning to end. But the villain has all kinds of different characteristics."

Vincent's work for Amicus came about as the result of his association with American International. He couldn't have known it at the time, but agreeing to do *The Fall of the House of Usher* for American International was another major turning point in his career, forever linking the names "Price" and "Poe." When I asked Price about this over lunch, he told me the deal came together rather quickly, especially since American International's executives were impressed with the track record his films had enjoyed:

"*House of Wax* had made a great deal of money compared to what it cost and I did several other films that made big profits as well. Jim Nicholson and Sam Arkoff at American International were aware of that. Roger Corman wanted to make some films based on Poe and the first was *The Fall of the House of Usher*. That part was right up my alley."

It must have taken all of Roger Corman's considerable persuasive talents to convince American International that it was time to splurge and shoot a horror film in color. He also talked the studio into providing enough money to hire Price, the name star he wanted for the adaptation he planned of the Edgar Allan Poe tale. The success of the film launched the series that followed.

"Danny Haller." That was the immediate response from Vincent Price when I asked him why these Poe films had such an expensive look despite relatively low budgets. Price didn't give me some magic formula or complicated budget-stretching trick ... just a name. Daniel Haller was the Art Director and Set Designer on the American International films. He had that all important quality that the studio valued so highly ... the ability to turn nothing into something. Here was a man who served as Art Director on such early shoestring productions as *The Ghost of Dragstrip Hollow*, *The Wasp Woman* and *Attack of the Giant Leeches*! By the time the Poe films came along he was adept at making small sets look large through careful design and the use of excellent matte work.

Price pointed out that American International never

actually had its own studio. "Mostly we used Producers Studio," he said. Producers had previously been called The California Studio and when I was there some 30 years ago it had changed its name to Raleigh Studios, which it still goes by as of this writing. It's one of the oldest studios in Hollywood and had long been a popular rental lot by the time American International got there. The studio got on the television bandwagon early, playing host to shows like *Superman*.

Daniel Haller saved time and money by getting staircases, balconies and other parts of sets from various studio scene docks.

The author exploring studio staircases for sets.

These economy moves actually helped create the overall illusion of opulence on many of the Poe films. An article in the October 1961 edition of *American Cinematographer*, describes Haller scouting the major studios for preconstructed units that could be put together to help form the sets he had already conceived for *The Pit and the Pendulum.* Haller found massive arches, fireplaces and doorways at Universal and located stairways and wall units at other studios. He'd have them delivered to California Studios and have the separate pieces assembled according to his floor plans.

Price began work with Roger Corman on *The Masque of the Read Death* near the end of 1963. This was Corman's first production in England and Daniel Haller came along to provide sumptuous-looking sets.

Shooting at Elstree gave Haller access to standing sets from the more expensive film *Becket*. Haller also utilized a monastery set from the comedy *Crooks in Cloisters*. The luxurious sets combined with the stellar cast that included Price, Hazel Court, Jane Asher, Nigel Green and Patrick Magee, gave the movie an extremely expensive look, and it has become a cult classic. Magee, of course, was in several Amicus films and Nigel Green appeared in *The Skull*.

While on the topic of set design in the British films of Vincent Price, I should mention that Price told me he was very impressed with Brian Eatwell's period sets for *The Abominable Dr. Phibes.* They added to the campy atmosphere of the film and Price said he had a great deal of fun shooting the movie.

He also told me that his role in the film, as a man seeking revenge against the doctors he believes were responsible for his wife's death, was another good example of why he preferred playing villains. As an actor playing a monster or madman, Price said, you get a chance to convey the circumstances that shaped the character: "They're usually kind of strange things, things that have happened to him. He usually wasn't born that way. Something has happened to him that has made him that way."

Price continued to appear in British-made films, and with good reason. There was an added financial benefit for Price when the actor shot a movie in England, and it resulted from American International's desire to make sure Price couldn't make horror movies for the competition. Sam Arkoff and Jim Nicholson realized the actor was a key ingredient in the success of their Poe films. But Vincent was freelancing and Poe's works were in public domain. That meant other producers, even Roger Corman, could bypass American International and film Poe projects of their own, if they could obtain Vincent's services. For that reason, American International put Price under contract. One of the advantages for the actor was the expense account he received when he was filming overseas.

In 1973, Ralph Edwards devoted an episode of his program *This Is Your Life* to Vincent. I interviewed Edwards a few years later, and although the show often seemed schmaltzy, Edwards was actually an extremely intelligent man who carefully researched the celebrities featured on the program, so that he could invite appropriate associates of those to be honored. American International's Sam Arkoff was among the guests on the tribute to Price and he began by stating something the actor had already told me. Arkoff signed Price for the simple fact that he knew his pictures usually made money. Arkoff went on to point out that Vincent had made many of his American International films in England. "And when in England," said Arkoff, "he gets a big fat expense account." Arkoff told Edwards that, periodically Price would claim the cost of living was going up in Britain and get an increase. "Now we all had illusions that Vinny was living like some Oriental Potentate in some deluxe London penthouse. But much to our surprise we discovered he was living in a modest room in a quiet hotel on a London side street. And the explanation? He was using most of his expense money to buy objects of art."

Even when American International shipped Price over to Europe for some embarrassingly bad films, the actor at least had the satisfaction of knowing that he was getting free transportation to international art centers. *House of 1000 Dolls* provided an opportunity to make art purchases in Spain and *Dr. Goldfoot and the Girl Bombs* gave Price a chance to visit the art galleries of Rome.

Italy and Spain may have been among the places the actor had in mind when I asked him one day to compare the technical abilities of crews in America and overseas:

"Britain and Hollywood are great for shooting, *especially compared to some of the other parts of the world where I've filmed.* One of the things about England is that the British crews are so welcoming. Technically, both Hollywood and Britain are so proficient and wonderful."

Sam Arkoff's contract with Price called for a certain

number of films in a certain period of time. If American International didn't have a project for the actor, the studio was willing to do a co-production deal with someone who did. That's how Vincent's first Amicus film came about. American International asked Milt Subotsky if he had anything that might be suitable for Price. Milt, always in the process of looking for stories to film, mentioned a book he had read called *The Disorientated Man.* American International liked the idea and the wheels were set in motion for the production of the film that would eventually be released as *Scream and Scream Again.*

The first time I spoke with Price was in a phone interview arranged by an influential columnist. The actor had just come back to Hollywood after filming *Theater of Blood* in Britain. We had a wide-ranging discussion that included questions about other films he had made in the recent past, including *Scream and Scream Again.* At this point that was the only film he had made for Amicus and I asked him what he thought of the company. Price was actually rather complimentary about Amicus, saying he liked the studio's style. And when we discussed Milton Subotsky's practice of hiring actors like Peter Cushing for as little as a day and Christopher Lee for two or three, he began to laugh and said: "Yes, I'm very aware of that .... the man is no fool!"

Indeed, Price was aware of Milton's method, since Subotsky had employed a variant of this formula in hiring Price for *Scream and Scream Again.*

Price looking sinister in *Scream and Scream Again.*

Milton arranged the schedule so that he only needed Price for two weeks, but agreed to pay him more than half of what he'd get for a regular shoot that could lasted four or five weeks. That meant Subotsky had enough money left in the budget to hire Lee and Cushing for brief appearances (in Cushing's case, *very* brief.)

Price was glad to be working in Britain at this point in his career. But he told me that, in the early days, he wasn't quite as enthusiastic about filming there.

"In the beginning I actually would have preferred to work near home. But I've done quite a few pictures in England now, and I must say they really do produce this kind of picture superbly."

Price said another reason he was in England so often was simply because an actor goes where the work is, and the work was in Britain:

"Both Hollywood and Britain are fun to film in. They are terribly, terribly good I must say, in Britain ... but I've simply been making pictures over here for the past several years because they haven't really been making as many of these types of pictures in Hollywood recently."

Luckily, Britain still had a few projects that were perfect for Price after *Scream and Scream Again*. In 1972, he was back with another camp performance in the inevitable *Dr. Phibes Rises Again*. Sequels are usually disappointing, but this one was a lot of fun.

Price told me he had even more fun making 1973's *Theater of Blood*. He said he enjoyed playing different characters in the film, as his angry Shakespearean actor attempts to murder leading critics with methods inspired by the Bard of Avon's plays. It isn't every horror film that provides someone of Vincent's talents with the opportunity to deliver Hamlet's soliloquy. And he told me there was also another reason he felt *Theater of Blood* was special:

"I was surrounded by so many great people ... Robert Morley ... the beautiful Diana Rigg and so many more. It's the kind of thing that you couldn't really do in Hollywood because you couldn't get all these distinguished actors over

from England at one time"

Robert Morley with Price in *Theater of Blood.*

Madhouse was hardly among Vincent's best films. At this point his contract with American International was ending, and Deke Heyward said, for Sam Arkoff, it was mostly about the deal, not the movie. Arkoff felt that, by partnering with Amicus or Tigon, if he could get enough money to cover Vincent's salary and a chunk of the production costs, he was well ahead of the game.

Director Jim Clark, who thought Subotsky was interfering, claimed later that Price felt the same way. That may well have been the case and I know there was some concern over the script for *Madhouse*. But not once did the actor ever say anything negative to me about Amicus or Milt Subotsky. Of course Price knew that I liked Subotsky, and he may not have said anything in front of me anyway. When I first spoke with Price about Amicus in 1972, he seemed quite positive about the company. Later, Price may have become somewhat less enthusiastic about Amicus, but I think that was part and parcel of his growing displeasure with American International. *Madhouse* was the last film under his contract with Sam Arkoff and he was happy to be rid of the deal.

But, when it came to the actual filming of the movie, it seemed to me that Price was quite comfortable. It was obvious from watching Price and Peter Cushing working together.

Anyone who has ever seen a movie being made can testify to the fact that it is often a boring and tedious process. That was not the case with *Madhouse*, largely because of the way Price and Cushing played off each other. And Price told me he was glad to occasionally be able to inject a little humor into his roles.

"I think many of the horror films I do these days really have more comedy to them, which is different from the old days."

The final film that Vincent Price would shoot for Milton Subotsky would contain perhaps too much comedy. *The Monster Club* (1980) wasn't officially an Amicus production, since Subotsky and Rosenberg had split by that time. But in addition to Price and John Carradine, veteran director Roy Ward Baker and former Amicus set designer Tony Curtis were on hand.

Milt's attempt at an omnibus horror film aimed at kids was uneven. It certainly wasn't a success when it was released, although it has developed a cult following in the intervening years.

The last time I saw Vincent Price he was getting ready to wrap up work on *Madhouse*, and I asked about his future plans:

"I'm going home, I'm going to be working in television and I've got a book I plan to finish ... I have a lot of things to do."

And it's not as if the actor's television schedule was light. Appearances on the small screen kept him very busy: "I'm on an average of 75 TV shows a year ... all types of shows, although I often find myself spoofing my horror persona."

Meanwhile, Price always seemed to be working on one writing project or another, often books about art or cooking. In fact, when we had spoken about a year earlier, he was putting the finishing touches on a book called "An American Treasury of Art." Much of that book had been written, he said, while he was flying back and forth to London to film movies. Price found writing was a great way to spend the otherwise boring time on long flights.

As he got older, Vincent Price felt the sadness of losing so many of his good friends.

"I was very close to Boris," Price said, "and I used to have so much fun with Basil Rathbone and Peter Lorre. Lon Chaney (Jr.) had been ill since the time I first knew him. But there were others I was close to, like Leo Carroll (Leo G. Carroll of *Topper*, *The Man from U.N.C.L.E.* and *Tarantula* fame.) It was sad when I learned of his passing."

Vincent had co-starred with Leo in the 1941 play *Angel Street*. Speaking about Carroll, Helen Hayes and others from his Broadway days, the actor sometimes seemed wistful about those years long ago when his name didn't automatically bring the idea of horror films to mind.

In most interviews he generally gave the impression that he really enjoyed being identified with fright films. I think that's true, but only to a certain extent.

In doing the research for this book, I went back to some of the original tapes which I hadn't heard in some 45 years. At one point on a tape I asked Price if he was concerned that his name had become so associated with "these types of roles" over the years. You hear him snap back rather testily,

"No more than it bothers John Wayne to be connected with westerns!"

What I actually meant by "these types of roles" was "villainous roles," not roles in horror films. When I quickly explained that, he went right back to his normal, cordial self. I have to say, though, that his initial response made me wonder how comfortable he really was with some of the films in which he appeared.

In the many years since my meetings with Vincent Price, I've often thought of something he said as we wrapped up one of our discussions. Looking back, I think it summed up his attitude toward a life he saw as quite fulfilling:

"I feel I'm very lucky, because I lecture on paintings and primitive art, write books and have an awful lot of other interests. I'm not just stuck with being an actor."

I'm sure all of us can agree that we feel very lucky that this talented man was "stuck with being an actor." Many of the films in which he appeared are all-time classics.

Vincent Price died in October of 1993. He was 82 years old and had continued acting almost up until the time of his death.

AMICUS AT SHEPPERTON

RKO, in its heyday, had three separate facilities in the Los Angeles area. RKO's Culver City lot alone encompassed 40-acres and had an administration building that resembled a southern mansion. Universal's founder Carl Laemmle built his studio on a 235 acre site, and constructed a complex so large that he could employ a virtual army of workers, many of them his relatives. MGM, in its glory days, had offices and sets sprawled out over 187 acres, along with its own police and fire departments, a full time landscaping staff and even its own post office. Amicus rented a couple of bungalows at Shepperton Studios in England.

The small space on the Shepperton lot served as the administration building, story development center, casting department ... virtually everything! What larger film companies spread over acres of land, Amicus handled in a little bit of rented space. There was room for a secretary, a small office for Milton and not much more ... hardly the headquarters of a typical movie mogul! The first horror film produced by the Max Rosenberg/Milt Subotsky partnership, *City of the Dead*, would be shot at Shepperton, even though the film would be attributed to Vulcan Productions. And their last horror film together, *The Beast Must Die*, would be shot there too, but under the Amicus banner.

20 years before Hammer would acquire Down Place and turn it into Bray Studios, an aspiring feature film producer named Norman Loudon bought a different mansion, Littleton Park, located on 60-acres in Shepperton, Surrey. The studio was successful and continued to expand, although filming was disrupted during World War II. Later, Sir Alexander Korda purchased a controlling interest in Shepperton.

But by the time Amicus arrived to shoot *City of the*

Dead, the studio was being run by British Lion. Actress Venetia Stevenson remembers *City of the Dead* being shot on the largest stage at Shepperton. That would be stage "H," which had plenty of room to create the spooky indoor village of Whitewood.

Subotsky must have been extremely impressed with the studio back in 1959. He would have learned of Shepperton's role in providing a suitable home for a long list of previous films, everything from *Sweeney Todd: The Demon Barber of Fleet Street* (1936) and *The Courtneys of Curzon Street* (1947) to *The Third Man* (1949) and *Room at the Top* (1958.)

The lot had already played host to a very young Hazel Court and Adrienne Corri in 1954's *Devil Girl from Mars*. Later, Monty Berman and Robert Baker used Shepperton for *Jack the Ripper* and *Flesh and the Fiends*, the latter staring Peter Cushing and Donald Pleasence. Production on *Ripper* began in late 1958, while *Flesh and the Fiends* began shooting in the spring of 1959 and Subotsky arrived in the fall.

Like *City of the Dead* the two Baker/Berman films concentrated on Shepperton's indoor sets, especially *Jack the Ripper* (below.)

!

For a company like Amicus, Shepperton was perfect. It had excellent facilities, modern sound stages, pre-and-post production services, scene docks, a large backlot ... everything that was needed for operation like Amicus, which co-founder Rosenberg once aptly described as "a studio without walls." Working at Shepperton also provided an opportunity for cooperation with other movie-makers. In a 1994 letter to *Filmfax* magazine, producer Richard Gordon ... the man responsible for such films as *The Haunted Strangler, Corridors of Blood* and *Island of Terror* ... told the following story: "Amicus was making one of its omnibus horror films at Shepperton Studios while I was shooting

Tower of Evil (a.k.a. *Horror on Snape Island*) there. On one occasion, Milton generously let us use some of his props when we needed them and in return, we let him use one of our standing sets for a short scene in his production."

Gordon said there were other ways producers on the lot were influenced by each other as well. Gordon was a fan of *City of the Dead,* and he knew George Baxt had written the screenplay for the movie. Gordon felt Baxt had done an excellent job on that film and it was Baxt who wrote the original story for Gordon's *Tower of Evil.* Also because of *City of the Dead,* he chose Desmond Dickinson as his cinematographer for *Tower of Evil.* Dickinson, who began his career as an assistant photographer in the late 1920's and graduated to director of photography by the 1930's, had been widely praised for the innovative way he shot *City of the Dead,* especially his success in emphasizing the eerie, fog-laden sets.

If there's anything everyone involved with the film remembers, it's that fog. It was created by using a kerosene spray fogger called "Nu Gel." It was deliberately kept at a temperature that would allow it to form a fairly high mist on the set as opposed to just swirling around on the floor of the stage. It's never easy trying to work around kerosene foggers, (Several actors complained they almost passed-out from the "Nu Gel" fumes while filming *Man from Planet X* on a small set at Hal Roach Studios a few years before) but director John Moxey said everyone involved with *The City of the Dead* was extremely cooperative.

When Milt Subotsky decided to find out if he could shoot his teen musicals on the British side of the pond, Shepperton was the logical choice. Not only had Shepperton worked out well for *City of the Dead,* but just prior to shooting the first British Amicus musical, *It's Trad, Dad,* the studio had gone through major renovations, including the construction of a new dubbing theater.

The Shepperton crew was also a plus for the 1962 Amicus musical. The director was Dick Lester who would soon gain fame with The Beatles. The cinematographer was Gilbert Taylor, who would go on to be director of photography on *A Hard Day's Night, Dr. Strangelove* and *Repulsion* and many other hit films. And dubbing editor Jim Shields would eventually work on *Alien* and most of the James Bond films.

While Subotsky was temporarily concentrating on music, Shepperton was playing host to several sci-fi and horror films. Movies like *The Day of the Triffids* (1962*)*, *The Black Torment*(1964), *Witchcraft* (1964) and *The Earth Dies Screaming* (1964), showed the studio was more than capable of providing creepy atmosphere, even when ... as was the case with *Triffids* ... the "monster" was supposed to be plant life. (The person who ran the fog machine at Shepperton would appear to have had a very secure job. In some scenes, to try to obscure the prop department origins of the

"Triffids", they pumped in almost as much fog as they used in *City of the Dead/Horror Hotel*!)

The Day of the Triffids may have inspired Amicus to think it could pull off a vegetation monster of its own at Shepperton, when it shot the "Creeping Vine" segment of *Dr. Terror's House of Horrors* (1965).

Vicious vine creeps up on Jeremy Kemp.

While *Vine* turned out to be one of the weaker links in the first Amicus omnibus film, overall the movie was a landmark for the studio. All the pieces were in place for the Amicus anthology films that would follow. We get the strong cast, headed by Peter Cushing and Christopher Lee, a simple but efficient framing device and atmospheric sets.

The sheer size of Shepperton's facilities came in handy for the next few Amicus productions. The studio provided accommodation for impressive indoor sets for *The Skull.* Director Freddie Francis even wore roller skates to get shots from the "Skull's" perspective.

And big sets were *really* needed for the *Dr. Who* films.

The next Amicus production at Shepperton, *Torture Garden*, needed mostly just the sound stages at the studio, and it was followed by four non-horror offerings: *Danger Route, The Birthday Party, Thank You All Very Much/A Touch of Love* and *The Mind of Mr. Soames*. Amicus got back into the horror domain at Shepperton with *Scream and Scream Again*, which would be followed by *The House that Dripped Blood.*

I promised in an earlier chapter to go into detail on some of the filming locations for *The House That Dripped Blood.* I think it's appropriate to do so here, because it sheds some light on Shepperton's suitability as headquarters for a creative independent filmmaker. Finding a studio with excellent facilities for indoor filming was one thing. But with Shepperton, a little ingenuity went a long way toward providing imposing outdoor locations as well. And if there was one thing Milton Subotsky had, it was ingenuity. An example: The large, spooky country house that formed the centerpiece of *The House That Dripped Blood.*

Subotsky loved to zip around Shepperton in a golf cart. It was the one luxury he allowed himself and you could tell it had nothing to do with wanting to play “big-shot” on the lot. Here was a guy who enjoyed movies and he simply liked to roam Shepperton checking out other productions that were filming while he was there. I liked the fact that I occasionally got a chance to tag along. I also got a chance to see the Subotsky ingenuity in action.

The first time I visited Shepperton, he took me over to one end of the property to see the original *House that Dripped Blood.* I assumed we were going to visit a false front, like so many other sets on the lot. I was wrong. Instead, the house that looked so foreboding on the screen was a real building, but much smaller than it appeared in the movie.

The *House That Dripped Blood* was, in fact, the old gatehouse at Shepperton. The main portico was still there but the elaborate windows from the film were gone. As I walked up to the windows with Milt, we looked inside and saw that the building was now filled with old lumber from discarded sets. It was rather sad to realize that the main framing device in *The House that Dripped Blood* was now being used as a storage building by Shepperton!

And it appeared that a large part of the house was missing! No, the building hadn't shrunk. It simply wasn't that large to begin with. Subotsky decided it would have to look bigger and more impressive for the film. And that wasn't the only problem. Milt told me the real gate for the original gatehouse was too close to the street and the distance to the house too short, to accommodate the long-shots of cars pulling up to the building. The picture below, from 1961's *On the Fiddle*, shows just how close the real gate was to the rather small building.

Subotsky tackled one problem at a time, beginning with

the less-than-impressive size of the gatehouse. He told me that he had Shepperton workers add a false front to the side of the building in order to make it look more imposing.

The overall effect is quite impressive. Milt used fake vines coming down the left front of the building to obscure the seam where the false addition joins the real building. Thank goodness he did, because without the addition, as you can see in the picture I took below, the whole building ended right where the wooden stairs begin.

I took this shot a little further back from the building and if you look closely you can see the real gate in the shadows on the extreme right. It was too close to the house on one side and up against a busy street on the other. Subotsky said he realized it simply couldn't be used.

In the end it was decided to build a false gate on the other side of the house opposite the real gate. That's the one the real estate agent stands in front of in the film and the one you see the cars passing through as unsuspecting renters arrive. Much of what you see in the photo below, except for the car, was the work of studio craftsmen. The gateposts and gates, and the entire part of the building on the right hand side, including the gargoyle and gothic window, were all additions.

Surrounding towns were also put to good use by Amicus. Shepperton is located less than a mile-and-a-half from Weybridge and Walton-on-Thames, both of which were handy locations for filming.

In *The House that Dripped Blood* there are several exterior scenes that were shot nearby. The Peter Cushing segment is the best example. The plot has Peter, trying to get over a woman he lost and finding what appears to be an image of her in a wax museum. He takes a walk to clear his mind, which takes him past a real-life pub in Weybridge.

And there are great shots of Peter, grieving for his lost love, thinking about her as he looks out over the water near the Weybridge-Lock sluice.

Peter then heads down into the center of town, where he passes an antiques shop. Across the street, he sees the mysterious wax museum that will form the centerpiece of this segment of the film.

Ironically, the exterior of the wax museum was, in real life, the warm and friendly "Weybridge Hall," used for catering and as a community gathering spot.

It should be noted though that, like so many of the sites mentioned in this book, both inside and outside studio lots, this one almost faced closure. Local officials wanted to save management fees by shutting it down, but a group called "Friends of Weybridge Hall" managed to win at least a temporary reprieve.

Unfortunately, the real-life *House that Dripped Blood* wasn't as lucky. It's long gone and so are the magnificent sets that adorned the original back lot of Shepperton. In the early seventies, John Bentley purchased Shepperton on behalf of Barclay Securities. The plan was to turn the studio into a high density housing development, but environmental concerns kept that from happening. Still, monetary pressures continued in the seventies and forced an auction of some of the studio's equipment and, eventually, the sale of a large chunk of the studio's property to developers.

But for most of the time Amicus was there, Shepperton remained intact. That was fortunate, since Amicus had to rely heavily on the studio's back lot for its next film, *I, Monster*. Back in 1968, Shepperton workers had created old London in all its glory for the award-winning movie *Oliver*. Two years later Milt Subotsky took advantage of the standing sets for *I, Monster*, directed by Stephen Weeks.

Lee, Weeks and Cushing on the old *Oliver* set

When I paid a visit to the back lot in 1972, the outdoor sets were a bit worse for wear. By now, the canvas used to replicate window curtains in *Oliver* and *I, Monster* was beginning to become torn and tattered. That meant, in some places, you could see directly through the "curtains" and realize that there was nothing behind them but scaffolding.

And it's true the sets were a bit shabby compared to their earliest days. The first shot below is from 1969. I took the second shot in 1972. You can use the clock in both pictures as a reference point.

The shop where Chris Lee steals a cane for his murderous rampage was still there, transformed into an art gallery.

And the streets where Lee used the cane were still there too.

Some of the sets Chris Lee roamed in *I Monster* were still pretty much the same when I was there and still could have been re-used without any problem.

Others were in need of some sprucing up.

For me, though, the backlot was magical. Of course, I had no way of knowing then that all this would one day be torn down to make way for "progress."

But there is a very attractive filming location that remains on the studio's grounds even today. Littleton Park House is part of the original estate. In *Asylum*, Amicus used New Lodge, near Windsor, to sub for the exterior of the mental institution. But Littleton Park House doubled for the interior.

It's fairly easy to spot Littleton Park House in movies. The paneled walls and parquet flooring tiles are distinctive.

Of course, the outside of the mansion is none too shabby either, and it got quite a bit of use in popular TV series over the years. *The Saint* and *Danger Man* (*Secret Agent* in the U.S.) are just two of the programs in which it appears.

Amicus used the exterior for *The Beast Must Die*, where

it's supposed to be a well-guarded mansion on an isolated island.

The mansion is, of course, right on the Shepperton backlot.

Shepperton played a major role in the Amicus story, serving not only as the company's headquarters, but also as the site of so many of its productions. These days Pinewood owns Shepperton, so it's part of a huge organization.

But I'll always remember Shepperton a little differently. I think of it as a place where magic took place every day. I remember visiting the plaster shop, where craftsmen were busy making everything from ornate statues to the fake tombstones used in Amicus horror pictures. I watched as men spread wet plaster over stretched burlap that could be turned into anything a set designer might want. Below is a shot I took of one very small corner of the huge storage area.

And as much as I admired Shepperton for its horror films, I was very aware of the fact that it was much in demand for a wide variety of other types of movies as well. That reality was brought home to me one day when Milt Subotsky took me over to see some of the stages used for *Tales from the Crypt* and other films. Before we jumped into his golf cart, he said he wanted me to see one of the biggest productions currently being shot on the lot, with stars like Peter Sellers and Dudley Moore. On this particular day one entire large stage was taken up with a set for the 1972 version of ... *Alice in Wonderland*!

Ah, the horror of it all ... *Alice in Wonderland* shooting alongside *Amicus in Horrorland*!

AMICUS AT TWICKENHAM

I didn't recognize the actress on the other side of the big spider terrarium in the middle of the *Madhouse* cellar set. She was in gruesome makeup and appeared to be pantomiming a scene she would be shooting when the crew got back from their break, so I didn't want to disturb her.

In order to stay out of the woman's way, I decided to spend some time exploring the rest of the set. To be honest, I'd already found the terrarium, with its plastic spiders and fake cobwebs, less than impressive. The woman had been holding one of the fake spiders in her hand and I didn't think it would fool anybody. I have to admit that I was also a little doubtful about the rest of the props.

There was a smaller room adjacent to the main set which was supposed to be filled with various hothouse plants and other greenery that didn't look very authentic either. I stood there in the middle of the fake plants and the phony plaster walls and windows and wondered how viewers could find any of this in the slightest bit realistic when the movie finally appeared in theaters.

When filming resumed after the break, the crew did add some real spiders for close-ups and I was also reminded of the talents of makeup artist George Blackler. He had worked on *Theatre of Blood, The Satanic Rites of Dracula, Dracula A.D. 1972, Twins of Evil* and *Lust for a Vampire*. Blackler was so good at his job that, I'm embarrassed to say, his work on *Madhouse* totally obscured the face of a woman I should have known, if only from the sheer number of films I had seen her in. Here was an actress who had appeared in genre favorites like *Devil Girl from Mars, Corridors of Blood, The Tell-Tale Heart, The Hellfire Club, A Study in Terror* and *Vampire Circus*. The woman I hadn't recognized earlier was the lovely Adrienne Corri, who was hidden under Blackler's heavy makeup when I first saw her.

In addition to not recognizing Adrienne, it turned out I didn't recognize the artistry of the talented people working on the sets for *Madhouse*. And when I finally did see the finished film, the sets looked quite spooky and rather lavish. I should have known this, of course, given the fact that Amicus regular Tony Curtis designed it and Ray Parslow, who was the cinematographer on *The House That Dripped Blood,* photographed it. The set appeared much larger and more realistic on the screen. And Amicus went on location to shoot exteriors, both at the docks along the Thames and on the extensive grounds of Pyrford Place in Surrey. It was for this type of filming that Twickenham Studios was ideal.

The studio was perfectly suited to productions that required mostly indoor sets. Founded in 1913, the facility would eventually become home to several Amicus productions initially consisted of just one stage. Despite the lack of elaborate facilities, by the thirties the studio was being used to film such genre favorites as *Juggernaut* with Boris Karloff and the Ivor Novello version of *The Lodger* (aka *The Phantom Fiend.*)

By the time Amicus began making films at Twickenham the studio was definitely a full service facility. The crews at Twickenham, like those at Shepperton, were usually quick and efficient. I witnessed that first hand once, when last-minute alterations were necessary just before the cameras were scheduled to roll. It was decided that a skeleton to be used in a Peter Cushing disintegration scene needed more blood. The crew quickly jumped into action, located some red paint and coated the prop with it in record time. (The gag shot below has me "interviewing" the skeleton while we waited for the paint to dry!)

The newly "bloodied" skeleton was ready in plenty of

time for the complicated scene, which required dissolve shots to have Peter morph into the skeleton.

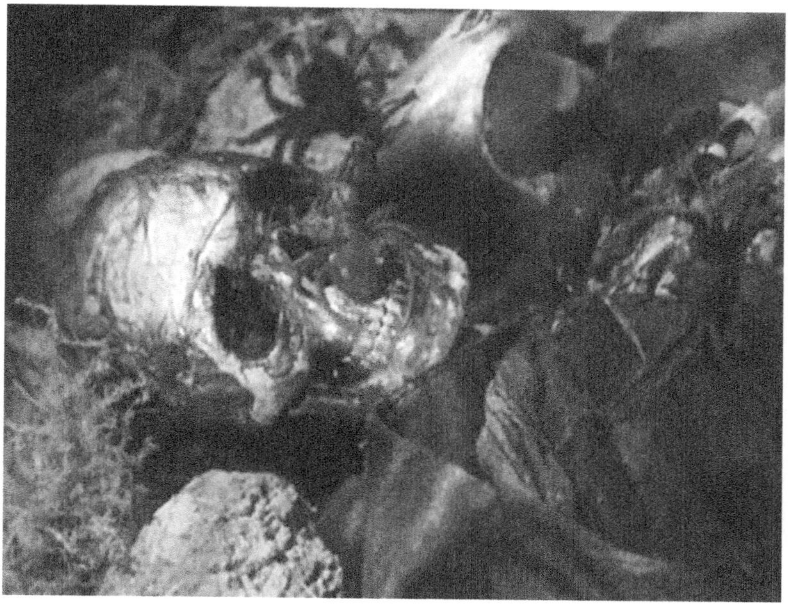

Twickenham was the perfect place to shoot a film like *Madhouse*. But Amicus didn't always used the studio to best advantage. In fact, in 1966 and '67, it seemed almost as if Amicus was deliberately taking projects it knew would be inferior and shunting them off to Twickenham.

The Deadly Bees was a case in point. The film involved very little location work and was quite stage-bound. Audiences had become more sophisticated. Yet Amicus used a stable courtyard that was obviously indoors as the setting for much of the movie's action.

The set, built on a Twickenham stage, was well constructed and showed attention to detail, but it was rather late in the day to expect audiences to fall for such artificiality. At one point, Michael Ripper, while fleeing from the bees, stumbles into a birch tree and it almost falls over! In short, the indoor sets used to represent the exterior of the bee-infested farm, gave the production an overall claustrophobic atmosphere.

But two other films Amicus produced at Twickenham made *The Deadly Bees* look like Academy Award material. “Cheap” is the only word to describe *The Terrornauts* and *They Came From Beyond Space*. Other studios, including Hammer, have tried the idea of making films back-to-back with some of the same personnel in order to save money. But few have had such disappointing results.

That isn’t to say *Terrornauts* and *Beyond Space* were totally without merit. It’s just that it was difficult for most viewers to see beyond the cheesy production values.

The two films were made for a combined budget that was less than what most studios would have spent on one film and, unfortunately, they looked it.

The “special effects” on both of these movies were anything but special, hardly capable of fooling children let alone adults. And the wardrobe department apparently searched rubbish bins for castoffs that could be used for the most laughable "space gear" possible.

At least *They Came From Beyond Space* did some location shooting, while *The Terrornauts* (below) mostly made do with cardboard sets.

While Twickenham didn't have a big back lot like

Shepperton, it did have some interesting nearby locations that were utilized by Amicus for some of its better films. One day, instead of driving to Twickenham, I went by rail. As I exited the St. Margaret's train station, I was surprised to see that the streets looked familiar. The station and the surrounding area were used in the Tom Baker segment of *Vault of Horror*.

Other locations for the movie, including the eerie,

vampire-infested town in the "Midnight Mess" segment with Daniel and Anna Massey, were in nearby Richmond. A laundromat called the *Washeteria* doubled as the outside of the vampire restaurant where Daniel finds himself on the menu. (Middle building below.)

The days of Milt Subotsky and Amicus shooting at Twickenham ended long ago. And the studio had a close call in 2012, when it was almost forced to close. But a buyer stepped in and revived Twickenham's fortunes.

It seems only fitting for the studio, with its rich history, to survive. And Amicus was part of that history. When Milt made It's *Trad, Dad!/Ring-A-Ding Rhythm*, he took a chance on a new director. His name was Richard Lester and Subotsky's teen musical gave him the opportunity to perfect the technique that would make him world famous when he directed The Beatles in *A Hard Day's Night*. By this time he was quite comfortable with Twickenham and used it again for the "Fab Four" film.

Twickenham's stages weren't as big as some of those at Shepperton, but they were big enough to accomplish what Amicus wanted to do. For me, Twickenham will always be remembered as the place where I enjoyed the warm and friendly company of the wonderful Peter Cushing. And also as the studio where, one day at lunch, Vincent Price's makeup put a major dent in my wife's appetite!

THE COMPLETE AMICUS FILM GUIDE
(Including Vanguard and Vulcan Films)

ROCK, ROCK, ROCK! (1956)

CREDITS: Producers: Max J. Rosenberg/Milton Subotsky; Director: Will Price; Screenplay: Milton Subotsky; Cinematographer: Morris Hartzband; Editors: Blandine Hafela, Robert Broekman; Production Company: Vanguard.

CAST**:** Tuesday Weld, Teddy Randazzo, Alan Freed, Fran Manfred, Jacqueline Kerr.

SUMMARY: This heart-felt drama tells the tragic story of Tuesday Weld's desperate search for the perfect dress for the school dance. In order to find an answer, lots of people have to sing lots of songs. In fact, virtually everybody but Tuesday winds up singing songs. Tuesday just moves her lips because Connie Francis dubs her voice! But she does get to dance.

MUSICAL PERFORMANCES: "You Can't Catch Me" (Chuck Berry); "I Never Had a Sweetheart," "Little Blue Wren" (Connie Francis dubbing Tuesday Weld); "I Knew from the Start," "Over and Over Again" (The Moonglows); "When It Comes to Love," "Give Me One More Chance" (Teddy Randazzo); "Would I Be Crying" (The Flamingos); "Tra La La" (LaVern Baker); "Rock, Rock, Rock," "The Big Beat" (Jimmy Cavallo and the Houserockers); "Rock Pretty Baby" (Ivy Schulman backed by Cirino and the Bowties); "Ever Since I can Remember" (Cirino and the Bowties);" Lonesome Train on a Lonesome Track" (The Johnny Burnette Trio); "Rock & Roll Boogie," "Right Now, Right Now" (Alan Freed's Rock & Roll Band with 'Big Al' Sears); "I'm Not a Juvenile Deliquent", "Baby, Baby" (Frankie Lymon and the Teenagers).

COMMENTS: Ah the teenage angst, as DJ Alan Freed holds a talent contest and brings his show to the school dance! On this rather slim frame hangs the foundation for *Rock, Rock, Rock!* But that isn't the point here...it's the music that's important. And the musical performances spotlighted in this film are a priceless time capsule of early rock!

JAMBOREE (1957)

CREDITS: Producers: Max J. Rosenberg/Milton Subotsky; Director: Roy Lockwood; Screenplay: Leonard Kantor; Cinematographer: Jack Etra; Editor: Anita Posner; Production Company: Vanguard.

CAST: Kay Medford, Bob Pastine, Freda Holloway, Paul Carr, Dick Clark.

SUMMARY: Will love find a way to bring Grace and Lew, two separated show-biz agents, back together again? Will the young and talented Honey and Peter have something to do with it? Will this all be an excuse to introduce a bunch of disc jockeys and a long list of great rock acts? The answer to all three questions: You bet!

MUSICAL PERFORMANCES: "Wait and See" (Fats Domino); "Hula Love" (Buddy Knox); "Crossover" (Jimmy Bowen); "Cool Baby" (Charlie Gracie); "Glad All Over" (Carl

Perkins); "Great Balls of Fire" (Jerry Lee Lewis); "Teacher's Pet" (Frankie Avalon with Rocco and His Saints); "Unchain My Heart" (Slim Whitman); "Sayonara" (Jodie Sands); "A Broken Promise" (The Four Coins); "One O' Clock Jump" (Count Basie); I Don't Like You No More" (Joe Williams backed by Count Basie) "Your Last Chance" (Lewis Lymon and the Teenchords); "Toreador" (Ron Corby A.K.A. Cauby Peixoto); "If Not for You" (Paul Carr); "Siempre," "For Children of All Ages" (Connie Francis); "Twenty-Four Hours a Day," "Who Are We to Say" (Connie Francis with Paul Carr) Note: Connie is once again stuck with dubbing duty.

COMMENTS: Few surprises here except for the great Jerry Lee Lewis, who gives us a rousing performance of an alternate version of his Sun Records hit "Great Balls of Fire."

It's nice to see Lewis' Sun label-mate Carl Perkins here too. Some rarely filmed rock pioneers are also featured, including Charlie Gracie and Buddy Knox.

THE LAST MILE (1959)

CREDITS: Producers: Max J. Rosenberg/Milton Subotsky; Director: Howard W. Koch; Screenplay: Milton Subotsky and Seton Miller. Cinematographers: Joseph C. Brun, Saul Midwall; Editors: Robert Broekman, Patricia Lewis Jaffe; Production Company: Vanguard

CAST: Mickey Rooney, Michael Constantine, Frank Overton, Ford Rainey, Don “Red” Barry, Clifford David, John Vari, Milton Selzer.

SUMMARY: A convicted killer (Rooney) joins several other men in the death house where they spend a lot of time talking until Mickey breaks out of his cell, frees the other guys and stages a standoff. The viewer knows this can’t possibly end well, and it doesn’t.

COMMENTS: Nothing wrong with this prison yarn, except that the story was pretty long-in-the-tooth by the time Rosenberg and Subotsky got around to filming it. It had been done as a play and then a movie in the early thirties. Mickey Rooney was the "name" in the cast, but he wasn't much of a "name" at this point in his career.

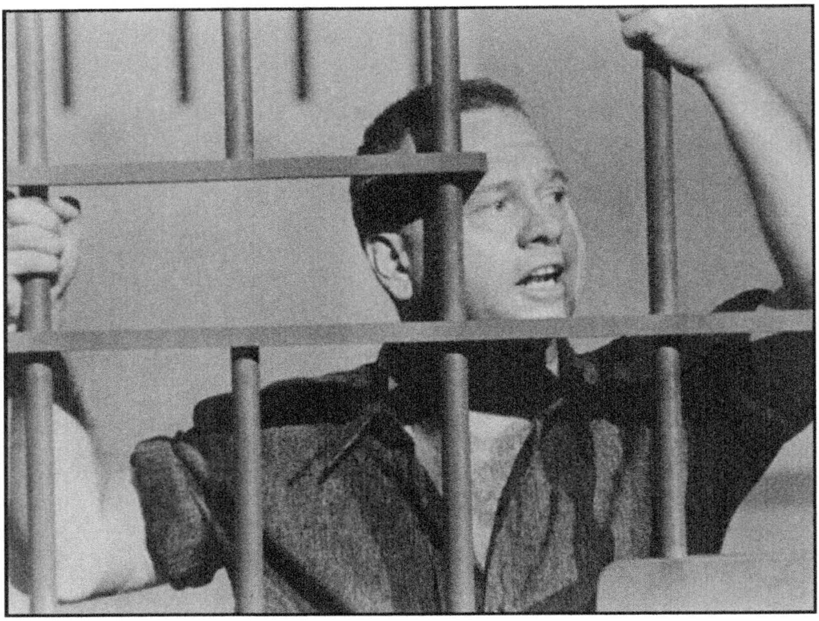

Watch for a very young Michael Constantine who would eventually star in *My Big Fat Greek Wedding*. It's also nice to see former western star Don "Red" Barry getting some work. And the film has a great jazz score similar to those used on the TV shows of the day like *M Squad* and *Johnny Staccato*. However this inexpensive black and white film with a B-list cast came out at a time when audiences were more interested in expensive color extravaganzas like *Ben-Hur* with Charlton Heston and *North by Northwest* with Cary Grant and Eva Marie Saint. So, while it received some good reviews, it didn't do big business at the box office.

CITY OF THE DEAD/HORROR HOTEL (1959)

CREDITS: Executive Producers: Seymour Dorner/Milton Subotsky; Producer: Max J. Rosenberg (uncredited): Director: John Moxey; Screenplay: George Baxt; Story: Milton Subotsky; Cinematographer: Desmond Dickinson; Editor: John Pomeroy; Production Company: Vulcan.

CAST: Christopher Lee, Patricia Jessel, Venetia Stevenson, Betta St. John, Dennis lotus, Tom Naylor, Valentine Dyal, Norman MacOwan.

SUMMARY: At your typical New England college a group of light-hearted students is taking a course on witchcraft from a professor, played by Christopher Lee. One of the students, played by Venetia Stevenson (below with Lee,) decides to spend part of her vacation in Whitewood, a village where Lee claims witches were burned at the stake.

Once you accept this premise and the fact that these American students keep slipping into British accents, fasten your seatbelts: You're in for one hell of a horror ride! Driving to the village, Venetia encounters a garage attendant who warns her away. And, after arriving at the village, the bushy-browed, gnarly-faced character actor Norman MacOwan, playing the elderly, blind Reverend Russell, urges her to "Leave Whitewood, Leave Whitewood tonight, I beg of you."

MacOwan as Reverend Russell: "Leave Whitewood."

But she pays him no heed because we wouldn't have a plot if she suddenly scurried home. Instead, she decides to remain in the fog-filled village to continue her research. When she signs-in to stay at the "Raven's Inn," which has been recommended by Lee, we can't help but notice that the innkeeper looks just like the witch that we saw being burned at the stake in the picture's prologue. All this leads to Venetia getting lured down to the cellar and killed by the witches who still inhabit Whitewood.

However, this is far too early in the game to lose our leading lady, so trusty stand-by heroine Betta St. John is called upon to step up to the plate.

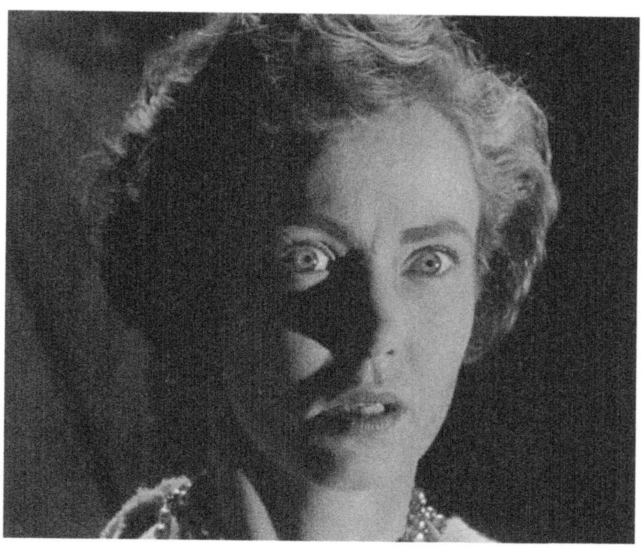

This is where the film really gets down to business, as Venetia's boyfriend and her brother attempt to discover the truth behind the mysterious goings-on. Viewers aren't likely to forget the powerful ending!

COMMENTS: Witches and fog, graveyards and fog, cobwebs and fog, human sacrifices and fog ... what's not to like? Actually, this is one of the better witchcraft movies made by any film company, let alone a low-budget one. It's definitely scary with great performances from Christopher Lee (who sports a pretty good American accent,) and the very frightening Patricia Jessel. This first venture into horror for the Subotsky/Rosenberg partnership was an impressive debut. Later films would benefit from color cinematography and bigger budgets, but the chill-factor of this initial effort stands the test of time.

GIRL OF THE NIGHT (1960)

CREDITS: Producer: Max J. Rosenberg; Director: Joseph Cates; Screenplay: Ted Berkman, Raphael Blau; Cinematographer: Joseph C. Brun; Editor: Aram A. Avakian; Production Company: Vanguard.

CAST: Anne Francis, Lloyd Nolan, Kay Medford, John Kerr, Eileen Fulton, James Broderick, Lauren Gilbert.

SUMMARY: Call girl Anne Francis is mistreated by her boyfriend/pimp John Kerr. He plays against type as a complete cad.

As often happened in in films made around this time period, it turns out fears that developed in childhood are keeping Anne tied to Kerr and to the oldest profession. Anne begins to see that her relationship with Kerr is just a continuation of her earlier mistreatment.

Psychiatrist Lloyd Nolan helps Anne see the truth.

COMMENTS: Milton Subotsky had been working on preparations for this film when he was sent to London to oversee *City of the Dead.* Subotsky received no credit on the film from Rosenberg, who simply listed himself as producer.

LAD: A DOG (1961)

CREDITS: Producer: Max J. Rosenberg; Directors: Aram Avakian, Leslie H. Martinson; Screenplay: Lillie Hayward, Roberta Hodes; Cinematographer: Bert Glennon; Editor: Tom McAdoo; Production Company: Vanguard.

CAST: Peter Breck, Peggy McCay, Carroll O'Connor, Angela Cartwright, Maurice Dallimore, Alice Pearce, Jack Daly, Charles Fredericks.

SUMMARY: Peter Breck and Peggy McCay own a courageous collie named Lad.

They have a wealthy neighbor who has a daughter stricken with polio. With this kind of set-up, it's inevitable that the plot will be designed to tug at the heartstrings and leave everybody walking out of the theater feeling better. But this really is a good film. The actors make all the difference. Breck and McKay are excellent and Angela Cartwright of *Lost in Space, Sound of Music* and *Danny Thomas Show* fame is perfect as the little girl who can't walk. Meanwhile, a pre-Archie Bunker Carroll O'Connor plays her father.

O'Connor, Maurice Dallimore, Cartwright, Lad.

Carroll O'Conner tries, but fails, to rig a contest so his dog will beat Lad. Then Lad saves O'Connor's daughter from a snake. Similar adventures follow.

COMMENTS: This was another project Milton Subotsky was getting ready for production when his partner shipped him over to London to get *City of the Dead* before the cameras. The cast is a good one, and the story should have appealed to kids, but the movie didn't perform all that well at the box office. Once again, Rosenberg failed to put Subotsky's name on the credits.

IT'S TRAD, DAD! / RING-A-DING RHYTHM (1961)

CREDITS: Producers: Milton Subotsky, Max J. Rosenberg (uncredited); Director: Dick Lester; Screenplay: Milton Subotsky; Cinematographer: Gilbert Taylor; Editor: Bill Lenny; Production Company: Amicus.

CAST: Helen Shapiro, Craig Douglas, Ronnie Stevens, Frank Thornton, Felix Felton

SUMMARY: Stop me if you've heard this one before: The oldsters in town are downright upset with the newfangled rock and updated Dixieland the kids are playing. The mayor is so incensed that he moves to shut down the local coffee shop where the music is played. Stars Helen Shapiro and Craig Douglas save the day, with a show that convinces everybody that this modern music is really cool!

Don't let the lack of a decent plot get in the way of enjoying

the innovations soon-to-be-famous Beatles director Richard Lester introduces in this movie.

MUSICAL PERFORMANCES: "She Never Talked About Me" (Del Shannon); "Let's Talk About Love" (Helen Shapiro); "Ring-A-Ding" (Helen Shapiro and Craig Douglas); "Rainbows" (Craig Douglas); "Seven Day Weekend" (Gary "U.S." Bonds); "Lose Your Inhibition Twist" (Chubby Checker); "Another Tear Falls" (Gene McDaniels); "Space Ship to Mars" (Gene Vincent); "Down by the Riverside," "When the Saints Go Marching In" (Ottilie Patterson); "Frankie and Johnny," "High Society," "In a Persian Market" (Acker Bilk); "Everybody Loves My Baby," "Dream Away Romance" (The Temperance Seven); "Double Trouble" (The Brook Brothers); "What Am I To Do" (The Paris Sisters); "Lonely City" (John Leyton); "My Maryland," "Tavern in the Town" (Terry Lightfoot) "By and By" (The Dukes of Dixieland) "Yellow Dog Blues" (Chris Barber's Jazz Band); "Beale Street Blues," "Nineteen Nineteen March" (Kenny Ball and His Jazzmen); "Aunt Flo," "Bellissima" (Bob Wallis and His Storyville Jazzmen) Note: Milton Subotsky receives composer credits on "Bellissima," "Space Ship to Mars," and "Frankie and Johnny."

COMMENTS: Essentially an updated version of the old Mickey Rooney/Judy Garland MGM musical plots, ("Hey Kids, let's paint the barn and put on a show that'll be the greatest this town has ever seen!") It's the pace set by director Richard Lester that makes this film so special ... almost like a rehearsal for his work with the Beatles. In his book *Rockerama,* British author Rob Burt called Richard Lester's direction of this film "hectic and zany," and said *It's Trad, Dad* contributed greatly to the energy, inventiveness and fast-paced humor of *A Hard Day's Night*.

JUST FOR FUN (1963)

CREDITS: Producers: Milton Subotsky, Max J. Rosenberg (uncredited); Director: Gordon Flemyng; Screenplay: Milton Subotsky; Cinematographer: Nicolas Roeg; Editor: Raymond Poulton; Production Company: Amicus.

CAST: Mark Wynter, Cherry Roland, Richard Vernon, John Wood, Jeremy Lloyd.

Cherry Roland, Mark Wynter, director Flemyng.

SUMMARY: Unhappy with older people in office, teenagers set up their own political party. They then get various rock acts to support them in the election. With "Doing the Hully Gully" for an anthem, how can this government possibly go wrong?

MUSICAL PERFORMANCES: "The Night Has a Thousand Eyes," "Touch Me") (Bobby Vee); "Up and Downs of Love," "I Gotta Get Up Early in the Morning" (Freddy Cannon); "Judy, Judy" (Johnny Tillotson); "Teardrops Fell Like Rain" "My Little Girl" (The Crickets); "Keep On Dancing" (Brian Poole and the Tremeloes); "All the Stars in the Sky" (The Tornados); "My Bonnie Lies Over the Ocean" (The Spotnicks); "Go" (Sounds Incorporated); "Crazy Crazes," "Monument" (Kenny Lynch); "The Man From Nowhere," "Hully Gully," (Jet Harris, Tony Meehan); "Happy With You," "Vote For Me," (Mark Wynter); "Just Another Girl" (The Vernon Girls); "Just For Fun" (Mark Wynter and Cherry Roland); "Little Boat" (The Springfields); "Let Her Go," "What's the Name of the Game?" (Joe Brown, below.)

Other songs in the film included "Warm Summer Day" (Ketty Lester); "Sweet Boy" (Clodagh Rodgers); and "Everyone But You" (Jimmy Powell.) Note: Milton Subotsky receives composer credits on "Everyone But You" and "Sweet Boy."

COMMENTS: There were two main factors working against *Just for Fun.* A) It was released just as the Beatles were taking the music world by storm and it didn't contain any Beatles music; B) It didn't have *It's Trad, Dad* director Richard Lester, who was about to become famous as the man at the helm of *A Hard Day's Night.* Gordon Flemyng was a serviceable director and worked later on the two Amicus *Dr. Who* films, but he couldn't add the quirky touches that made Lester's musicals stand out. As to the lack of Beatles music in the movie, it was the kiss of death. The Liverpool group swept everyone else off the charts. Even a pop idol like Bobby Vee, who had a major hit with "The Night Has a Thousand Eyes," heard in this film, would go through a long dry spell.

Vee wouldn't return to the charts until 1967 when he had a hit with "Come Back When You Grow Up Girl." But for others in *Just for Fun*, like Freddy Cannon, the hits were pretty much finished.

Dusty Springfield appears, but as part of The Springfields. She wouldn't become a superstar until she went solo.

The box office results were disappointing. And, thankfully for horror fans, that got Amicus moving in another direction.

DR. TERROR'S HOUSE OF HORRORS (1965)

CREDITS: Producers: Milton Subotsky, Max J. Rosenberg (uncredited); Director: Freddie Francis; Screenplay: Milton Subotsky; Cinematographer: Alan Hume; Editor: Thelma Connell; Production Company: Amicus.

CAST: Peter Cushing, Christopher Lee, Michael Gough, Bernard Lee, Donald Sutherland, Neil McCallum, Jennifer Jayne, Kenny Lynch.

SUMMARY: Whatever you do, don't let Peter Cushing read your fortune! Nobody's future looks too bright in this one. Neil McCallum returns to his ancestral house in Scotland and proves you really can't go home again ... unless, of course, you don't mind running into a werewolf. McCallum, (with Peter Madden, below) decides to melt the crucifix he's holding into silver bullets.

Unfortunately, by the time McCallum discovers the true identity of the werewolf, it's too late.

The next two tales starred Alan Freeman and Roy Castle, shown below taking a break on the set.

Freeman's segment, *The Creeping Vine,* comes next and the title pretty much says it all. He has to contend with some frightening foliage and, even with help from Bernard Lee ("M" in the James Bond films,) he can't win.

Freeman and Lee try fire on the vine at the door

In the next tale, Roy Castle gets his just deserts when he learns the hard way that stealing tunes from Voodoo ceremonies is a no-no. This segment is a favorite with many music fans because it contains tunes by jazz great Tubby Hayes and the Russ Henderson Steel Band. The plot is a simple one: Castle and his band get a booking in the West Indies. They sneak into a Voodoo ceremony and Castle is dumb enough to get caught writing down the notes to a sacred voodoo tune. Of course, he builds an act around the piece of music as soon as he gets back and the native gods are not happy. Castle's fate is foretold in Peter Cushing's Tarot cards.

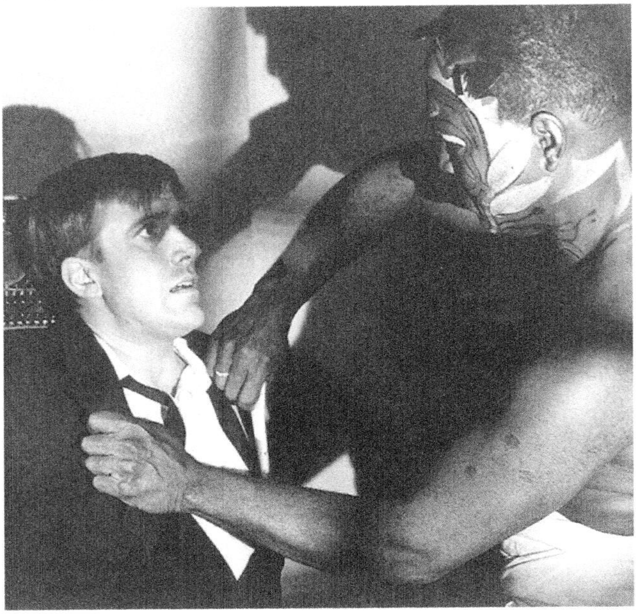

Next, Christopher Lee plays a pompous art critic haunted by Michael Gough's severed hand.

Gough is an artist who, tired of Lee's bullying, humiliates the critic by tricking him into giving a rave review to a painting done by a chimp. Lee retaliates by running over the artist with his car. Gough loses his hand in the hit and run and, knowing he will never paint again, kills himself. But, in the end, Gough's disembodied hand evens the score. By the way, this same mechanical hand shows up in several other Amicus movies.

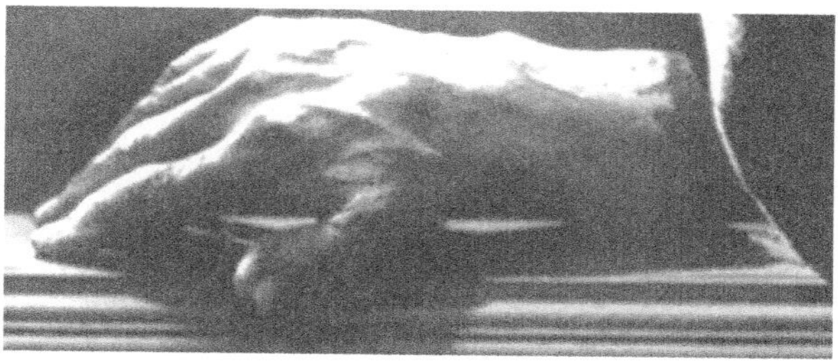

The final segment of the film has Donald Sutherland bringing home a lovely young woman who, unfortunately, turns out to be a vampire.

Donald Sutherland and Jennifer Jayne

Of course his wife isn't necessarily the only vampire in town, as Donald finds out.

Max Adrian and Donald Sutherland

COMMENTS: This is the one that provided the cornerstone for the studio's reputation as "Home of the Anthology Horror Film." The project was one Subotsky had been hoping to launch for a long time. The elements were all in place: A great cast, impressive color cinematography, good stories and a simple but effective framing device. Christopher Lee referred to it as "...an intelligent and absorbing film with an excellent cast" in "The Films of Christopher Lee" by Robert W. Pohle Jr. and Douglas C. Hart. The movie established Amicus as a studio that could give Hammer a real run for the money and the final shot of "Dr. Terror" still provides a chill after all these years!

THE SKULL (1965)

CREDITS: Producers: Max J. Rosenberg/Milton Subotsky; Director: Freddie Francis Screenplay: Milton Subotsky (From a short story by Robert Bloch); Cinematographer: John Wilcox; Editor: Oswald Hafenrichter; Production Company: Amicus.

CAST: Peter Cushing, Christopher Lee, Nigel Green, Patrick Wymark, Patrick Magee, Jill Bennet, Michael Gough.

SUMMARY: The skull of the Marquis De Sade is very popular. Christopher Lee had it, Patrick Wymark stole it and Peter Cushing wants it. But, in the end, it is Cushing who gets the skull, or...more accurately...the skull gets him!

COMMENTS: An excellent cast and good production values work in the film's favor, and so does ... believe it or not .... a script Milt Subotsky wrote that came in too short. Director

Freddie Francis had to bring the film up to time by adding some inventive twists. He even lets us see some of the action from the skull's perspective.

Subotsky must have done quite a job negotiating salaries on this one. He was trying to spend no more than £100,000 on the film, yet he managed to get a cast that included Peter Cushing, Christopher Lee, George Coulouris, Nigel Green, Patrick Magee, Michael Gough and Patrick Wymark.

Patrick Wymark, Peter Cushing and friend

DR. WHO AND THE DALEKS (1965)

CREDITS: Producers: Max J. Rosenberg/Milton Subotsky; Director: Gordon Flemyng Screenplay: Milton Subotsky (From a story by Terry Nation); Cinematographer: John Wilcox; Editor: Oswald Hafenrichter; Production Company: Amicus/AARU.

CAST: Peter Cushing, Roy Castle, Jennie Linden, Barrie Ingham, Roberta Tovey, Geoffrey Toone, Michael Coles, John Brown.

SUMMARY: Dr. Who, his granddaughters Susan and Barbara and Barbara's boyfriend Ian, take off by accident in the good doctor's time machine. They wind up in a strange world populated by good guys (The Thals,) and bad guys (The Daleks.) Dr. Who and crew help the Thals triumph.

Susan (Roberta Tovey) with Peter Cushing

The film reunited Peter with Roy Castle, who had appeared in *Dr. Terror's House of Horrors*.

COMMENTS: The right film at the right time. The BBC television series was a huge hit and viewers were hungry for a big-screen color version. Some fans were disappointed that Peter's Dr. Who was different from the television version, but overall the film did well, which meant that Peter could look forward to another Dr. Who movie in the not-too-distant-future.

THE PSYCHOPATH (1966)

CREDITS: Producers: Max J. Rosenberg/Milton Subotsky; Director: Freddie Francis, Screenplay: Robert Bloch; Cinematographer: John Wilcox; Editor: Oswald Hafenrichter; Production Company: Amicus.

CAST: Patrick Wymark, Judy Huxtable, Alexander Knox, Margaret Johnson, Thorley Walters, John Standing, Colin Gordon.

SUMMARY: The police are confronted with a dead body and a doll lying next to it that looks just like the victim...then another body, and another ... always accompanied by a doll. Not to worry, detective Patrick Wymark is on the case.

Patrick Wymark holds a doll of one of the victims

The common thread in the murders is discovered and it leads to a slightly batty family complete with a neurotic son and a crippled mother, played by Margaret Johnston, who just happens to collect dolls.

COMMENTS: The movie had a lot of positives. It was scripted by Robert Bloch, had a cast of solid actors, and the talented Freddie Francis as the director.

Director Freddie Francis with Judy Huxtable.

The film did well at the box-office, but it wasn't a huge hit, perhaps because it's more "who-done-it" than "horror."

DR. WHO AND THE DALEKS (1966)

CREDITS: Producers: Max J. Rosenberg/Milton Subotsky; Director: Gordon Flemying Screenplay: Milton Subotsky (From a story by Terry Nation); Cinematographer: John Wilcox; Production Company: Amicus/AARU.

CAST: Peter Cushing, Bernard Cribbins, Andrew Keir, Jill Curzon, Roberta Tovey, Ray Brooks, Geoffrey Cheshire.

SUMMARY: Once again, Dr. Who's time machine takes off by mistake, although you'd think after his last adventure he would have installed a safety lock. This time around the doctor is joined by Bernard Cribbins instead of Roy Castle, and Jill Curzon rather than Jennie Linden. But Roberta Tovey is a familiar face and the general plot is a bit familiar too.

Cribbins, Cushing, Curzon, and Tovey.

Transported into the future, they again find bad guys in the form of the Daleks and good guys in the form of people valiantly trying to fight the Daleks.

Cribbins and Peter look worried, but just in time we get the happy ending we've all been waiting for!

COMMENTS: Another excursion into the world of Dr. Who, as the earth faces peril amid some fairly decent matte shots and special effects. Although not as successful as the first film, the movie scored with its youthful target audience.

THE DEADLY BEES (1967)

CREDITS: Producers: Max J. Rosenberg/Milton Subotsky; Director: Freddie Francis; Screenplay: Robert Bloch (Partially rewritten by Anthony Marriott); Cinematographer: John Wilcox; Editor: Oswald Hafenrichter; Production Company: Amicus.

CAST: Suzanna Leigh, Frank Finlay, Michael Ripper, Guy Doleman, Catherine Finn, John Harvey, Michael Gwynn, James Cossins, Katy Wild.

SUMMARY: Suzanna Leigh, a singer who has been working too hard, is ordered by her doctor to take some time off. As so often happens in this type of film, Suzanna winds up in the worst of all possible places for a vacation ... an isolated farm where a homicidal maniac is using specially bred bees to kill off the locals. Suzanna, who looks very good in a bra and a half-slip, is afraid.

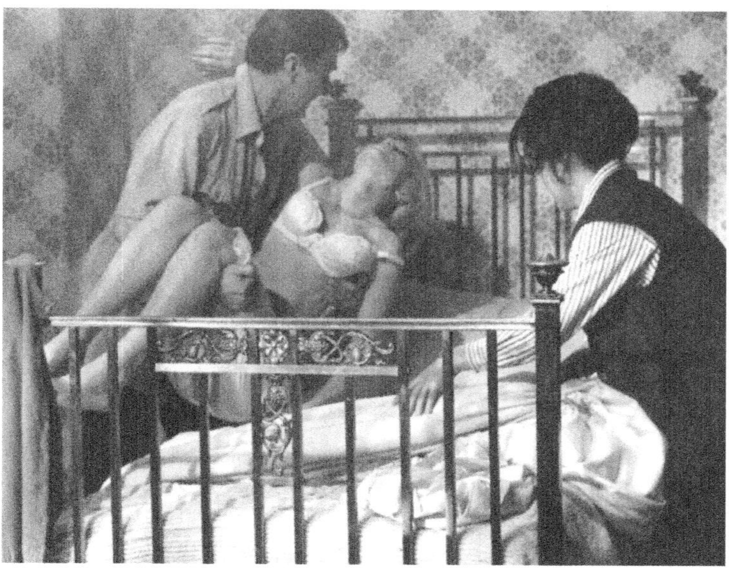

Suzanna being put to bed after bee scare

But she has her suspicions about the culprit, and spends the rest of the movie investigating. She of course turns out to be totally wrong and the least likely suspect, who alert viewers will have spotted early on, turns out to be the bad guy. Not to worry, though, as I may have mentioned Suzanna looks very good in a bra and a half-slip. While the special effects when the bees attack were rather pathetic, the original makeup *after* the bees attack Catherine Finn (Michael Ripper's real-life wife,) was quite good.

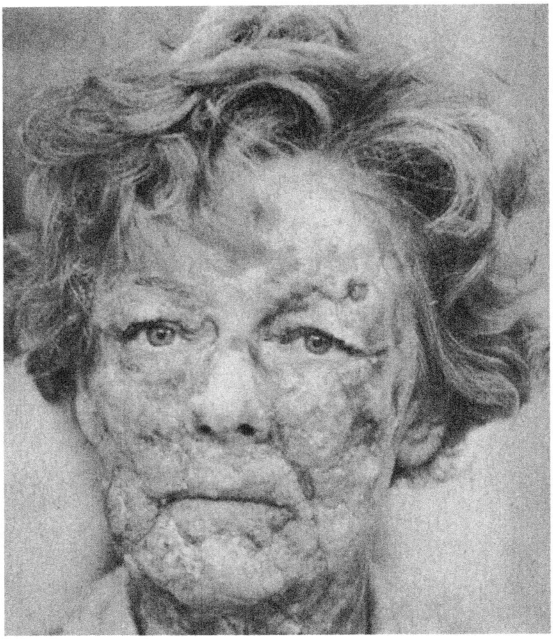

COMMENTS: An early example of truth-in-advertising, since the word "Deadly" appears in the title. Robert Bloch was hired to write the screenplay but someone else did a rewrite, and Bloch didn't think much of the finished product. Moviegoers apparently agreed. But it is nice to see Hammer regulars Michael Ripper and Michael Gwynn in this Amicus film and Suzanna would go on to appear in such Hammer offerings as *The Lost Continent* and *Lust for a Vampire.*

THE TERRORNAUTS (1967)

CREDITS: Producers: Max J. Rosenberg/Milton Subotsky; Director: Montgomery Tully, Screenplay: John Brunner; Cinematographer: Geoffrey Faithfull; Editor: Peter Musgrave (uncredited); Production Company: Amicus.

CAST: Simon Oates, Zena Marshall, Max Adrian, Patricia Hayes, Stanley Meadows, Charles Hawtrey, Richard Carpenter.

SUMMARY: Scientists in Britain, who've been trying for years to communicate with other planets, finally get some signals from outer space. Unfortunately, there's no time to celebrate, because they're promptly kidnapped by an alien spaceship. The trappings for this film are a tad threadbare. The "monster," with Zena Marshall below, looks like a poor man's "Jolly Green Giant" on a bad hair day.

Soon, the earthlings are undergoing intelligence tests administered by a robot. As our happy little crew endures further adventures, it becomes clear that the robot should have given the scriptwriter an intelligence test before this thing was filmed!

COMMENTS: Amicus tried something that even Roger Corman had refused to do anymore for American International. Corman no longer made two black and white movies for two-hundred thousand dollars. Instead, he put the two-hundred thousand into one, better quality, color film. Now, seven years later, Amicus thought it could make two films *in color* for approximately 200-thousand. *The Terrornauts* and the film that followed proved you could make them for that price, as long as you didn't worry about silly little extras like plot, special effects and production values. It appears the wardrobe department was especially hard hit.

How embarrassing for Simon Oates and his fellow cast-members. Let's face it. Attaching a few wires to an elastic beanie does not make it look like the latest in cutting-edge scientific headgear!

THEY CAME FROM BEYOND SPACE (1967)

CREDITS: Producers: Max J. Rosenberg/Milton Subotsky; Director: Freddie Francis; Screenplay: Milton Subotsky; Cinematographer: Norman Warwick; Editor: Peter Musgrave; Production Company: Amicus.

CAST: Robert Hutton, Jennifer Jayne, Michael Gough, Bernard Kay, Zia Mohyeddin, Maurice Good, Geoffrey Wallace, Paul Bacon.

SUMMARY: Okay, so here's the deal: What appears to be a group of flashlights flying in V-formation crashes into a field in Britain. But we're supposed to believe they're actually a shower of meteorites. Scientists investigating the incident are taken over by a mysterious force that makes them act like robots. (Actually the rest of the cast mostly acts like robots too, but why be picky?) Robert Hutton, who seems never to have turned down an Amicus script, has a friend who can break the spell by wearing an upside down salad strainer on his head.

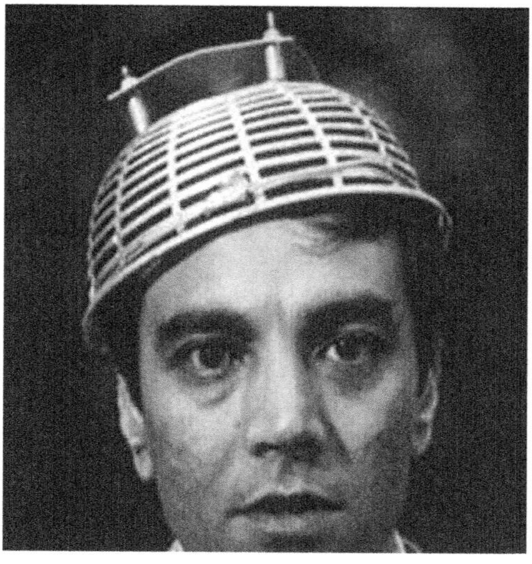

This is space-age headgear?

Anyway, Hutton and friends steal away on a rocket ship miniature that looks suspiciously like a Revell model kit, and meet alien leader Michael Gough. Michael tells them he's only been grabbing earthlings because his people need help repairing one of their ships that has crashed on the moon. "Oh, is that all," say the earthlings. "We'll be happy to help ... there's no need to kidnap us!" Michael and his crew, wearing shower curtain capes with Christmas tree skirts for collars, are very relieved.

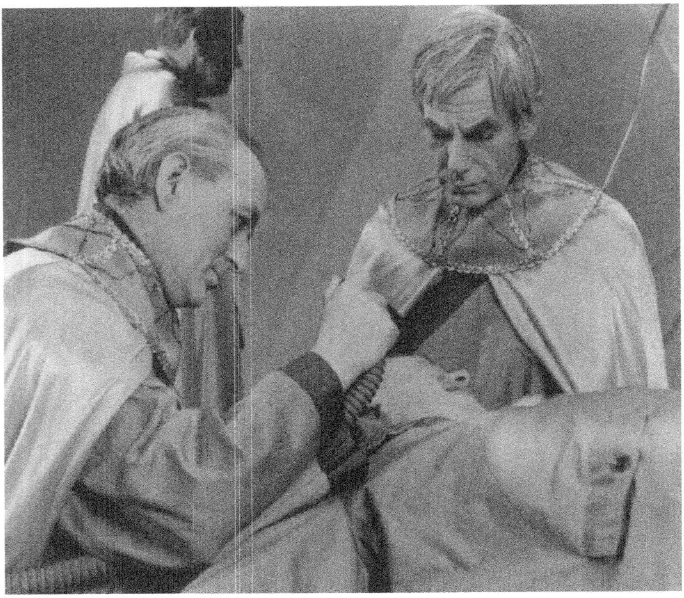

The camera zooms in on Hutton and Gough shaking hands, and superimposed on the touching scene we see the words: "The End ... Made at Twickenham Film Studios."

COMMENTS: Think *Plan Nine from Outer Space* only in color. Not even Freddie Francis could save it. Your heart goes out to the poor actors who had to slog their way through this mess. The only lucky one was Michael Gough, who couldn't have worked more than a day on it, since he only shows up for a few minutes at the end!

TORTURE GARDEN (1967)

CREDITS: Producers: Max J. Rosenberg/Milton Subotsky; Director: Freddie Francis, Screenplay: Robert Bloch; Cinematographer: Norman Warwick; Editor: Peter Elliott; Production Company: Amicus.

CAST: Peter Cushing, Jack Palance, Burgess Meredith, Beverly Adams, John Standing, Michael Bryant, Robert Hutton, Michael Ripper, Barbara Ewing, Maurice Denham.

SUMMARY: In *Torture Garden*, Burgess Meredith reveals the dark fortunes of visitors to a carnival sideshow.

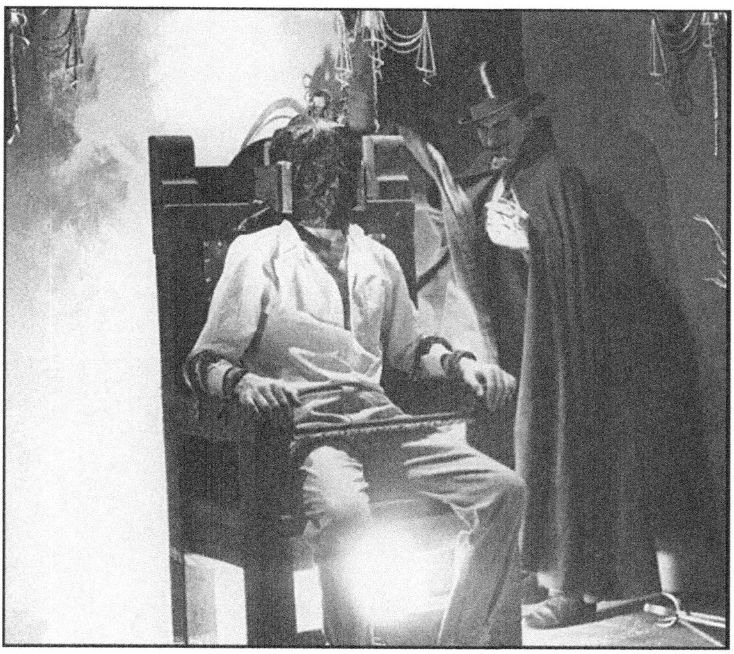

In the stories Meredith tells, Michael Bryant kills his uncle, starlet Beverly Adams has an affair with actor Robert Hutton, and Barbara Ewing falls in love with talented pianist John Standing, all with unexpected consequences. And, in the best segment, old pros Peter Cushing and Jack Palance play obsessive Edgar Allan Poe collectors. Peter has a Poe that Jack wants, so Jack kills Peter. Only then does Palance discover that Peter didn't have *a* Poe, he had *the* Poe!

There's a final twist in the framing story of this film and it involves our old friend Michael Ripper.

COMMENTS: This movie returned Amicus to the anthology format and it seemed things were back on track. But it was not to last.

DANGER ROUTE (1967)

CREDITS: Producers: Max J. Rosenberg/Milton Subotsky; Director: Seth Holt, Screenplay: Meade Roberts; Cinematographer: Harry Waxman; Editor: Oswald Hafenrichter; Production Company: Amicus.

CAST: Richard Johnson, Carol Lynley, Barbara Bouchet, Sam Wanamaker, Harry Andrews, Diana Dors, Sylvia Syms, Gordon Jackson, Maurice Denham, David Bauer.

SUMMARY: Richard Johnson, who was originally a favorite for the role of James Bond, plays a spy of a different kind in this movie. He'd really like to get out of the spy business, but he's told he must complete one last assignment. In the course of doing so he'll uncover a double agent and eventually unveil an ending that may surprise you. He'll also romance some lovely ladies, like Carol Lynley (below).

COMMENTS: For horror fans Richard Johnson will always be best remembered as Dr. John Markway in 1963's *The*

Haunting with Julie Harris. *Danger Route* was a departure for Amicus, but it's a good spy film. It's just that the public was more interested in James Bond and his gadgets at the time, than in Johnson and his karate chops.

By the time *Danger Route* reached theaters, television had already been presenting very similar fare. Patrick McGoohan's *Danger Man*, known in the U.S. as *Secret Agent,* included several episodes directed by Seth Holt, who helmed this film. Holt directed *Scream of Fear*, *The Nanny*, and *Blood from the Mummy's Tomb* for Hammer. Many of the cast members in *Danger Route* will be familiar to Amicus fans. Richard Johnson had a long career and worked for Milt Subotsky once again in *The Monster Club*. I had the pleasure of watching Diana Dors, who appears here as Rhoda Gooderich, when she was shooting *From Beyond the Grave*. Sylvia Syms was excellent in Asylum and Maurice Denham appeared in *Torture Garden*.

THE BIRTHDAY PARTY (1968)

CREDITS: Producers: Max J. Rosenberg/Milton Subotsky; Director: William Friedkin, Screenplay: Harold Pinter; Cinematographer: Denys Coop; Editor: Antony Gibbs; Production Company: Amicus.

CAST: Robert Shaw, Patrick Magee, Dandy Nichols, Sydney Tafler, Helen Fraser, Moultrie Kelsall.

SUMMARY: Robert Shaw is staying in a boarding house by the sea. Would that there was a menacing shark around, but Shaw wouldn't star in Steven Spielberg's *Jaws* for another 8 years, so we're stuck with a Harold Pinter script that's wordy and boring or bold and provocative, depending on individual taste.

COMMENTS: Grasping defeat from the jaws of victory, Amicus failed to follow up on the success of *Torture Garden* or even the more modest performance of *Danger Route* and instead, produced three less profitable but more "artsy" films in a row. The movie was extremely faithful to the play, perhaps too much. On the other hand, the film gave viewers a close look at young Robert Shaw's abilities as a serious actor and showcased Patrick Magee as well.

The Birthday Party gave Amicus bragging rights to bringing a Harold Pinter play to the screen but that failed to translate into big box office returns.

THANK YOU ALL VERY MUCH / A TOUCH OF LOVE (1969)

CREDITS: Producers: Max J. Rosenberg/Milton Subotsky; Director: Waris Hussein, Screenplay: Margaret Drabble; Cinematographer: Peter Suschitzky; Editor: Bill Blunden; Production Company: Amicus.

CAST: Sandy Dennis, Ian McKellen, Eleanor Bron, John Standing, Rachel Kempson, Michael Coles, Kenneth Benda, Maurice Denham, Peggy Thorpe-Bates, Sarah Whalley.

SUMMARY: Sandy Dennis, a graduate student surrounded by other upwardly-striving young people, finds herself pregnant. The movie follows her new life as an unwed mother, as we wait to see whether she will reunite with the baby's father or choose to live alone.

COMMENTS: The story may seem old hat today, but it was controversial at the time and the film was well done. The biggest problem watching *Thank You All Very Much* today is trying to concentrate on the movie itself rather than being diverted whenever Ian McKellen is in a scene with Sandy.

He appears so young compared to the Ian McKellen we came to know in the years since this film was made, that it seems almost as if we're looking at two different people.

The film's overall box office returns were disappointing.

THE MIND OF MR. SOAMES (1970)

CREDITS: Producers: Max J. Rosenberg/Milton Subotsky; Director: Alan Cooke, Screenplay: John Hale, Edward Simpson; Cinematographer: Billy Williams; Editor: Bill Blunden; Production Company: Amicus.

CAST: Terence Stamp, Robert Vaughn, Nigel Davenport, Donal Donnelly, Christian Roberts, Dan Jackson, Norman Jones, Judy Parfitt, Vickery Turner.

SUMMARY: Terence Stamp has been in a coma since infancy. An operation performed by neurosurgeon Robert Vaughn brings him out of the coma, but he exists as a child in an adult body. Scientist Nigel Davenport wants to greatly accelerate the learning process for Stamp. But Vaughn feels it's important that Stamp have at least a taste of childhood and shows him how to play with things like slot cars.

COMMENTS: Another side-trip for Amicus, this time into territory that had been covered more successfully in the Cliff

Robertson film *Charly* two years earlier. *The Mind of Mr. Soames* veers between sci-fi, fantasy and melodrama and the ending leaves a lot of questions unanswered. But even under the direction of Alan Cooke, who worked mostly in television, Terrence Stamp does a fine job.

Cooke and Stamp take a break

Shot at Shepperton, the overall "look" of this film is excellent. The talented Billy Williams was among those who worked on it and he would go on to serve as director of photography on such films as *Sunday Bloody Sunday*, *Voyage of the Damned*, *On Golden Pond*, and *Gandhi*. Yet, like the other attempts by Amicus to break the mold and improve the image of the company, *The Mind of Mr. Soames* was a disappointment at the box office when it was first released. The movie's reviews were mixed, perhaps because some objected to the film's inconclusive ending. Hard to find for many years, now that it's become more widely available it's beginning to develop a cult following.

SCREAM AND SCREAM AGAIN (1970)

CREDITS: Producers: Max J. Rosenberg/Milton Subotsky; Director: Gordon Hessler; Screenplay: Christopher Wicking; Cinematographer: John Coquillon; Editor: Peter Elliott; Production Company: Amicus.

CAST: Vincent Price, Christopher Lee, Peter Cushing, Judy Huxtable, Christopher Matthews, Michael Gothard, Anthony Newlands, Kenneth Benda, Uta Levka, Yutte Stensgaard.

SUMMARY: Get out your secret decoder rings, because you may need them to follow this plot! No wonder Vincent Price said he never understood this movie. At the beginning, a man wakes up in a hospital-type bed and sees that his leg is missing.

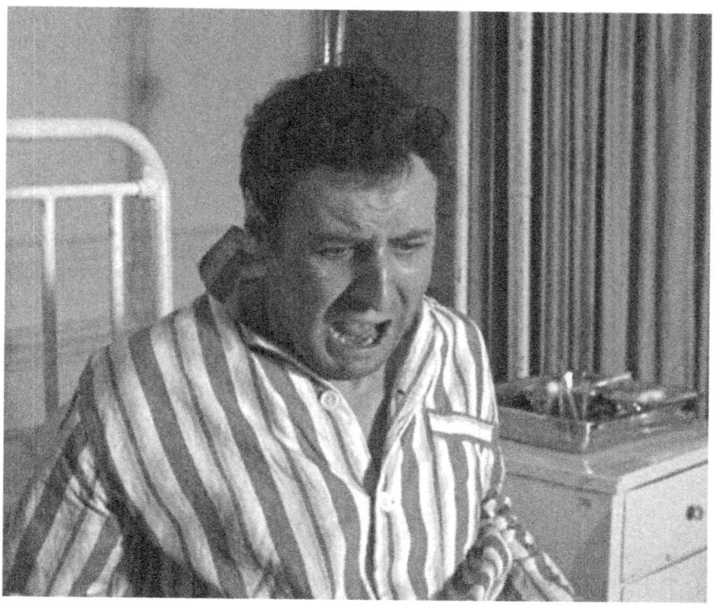

Next, death lurks in a Nazi-like foreign landscape before the film switches to a sex crime in Britain. There are lots of other scenes that don't seem to hang together either, until we finally realize late in the film that it's really all about the creation of humanoids. There's even an *Invasion of the Body Snatchers* type twist at the end!

COMMENTS: At long last Amicus took a break from message movies and returned to the horror milieu. With Gordon Hessler at the helm and American International involved, the film has a different look from the typical Amicus effort.

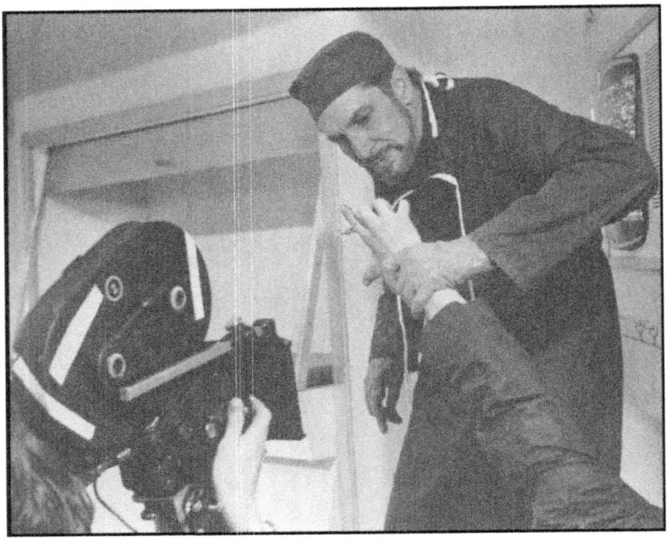

But Milt Subotsky did find a way to work his favorite severed hand into the picture, this time attached to a car bumper.

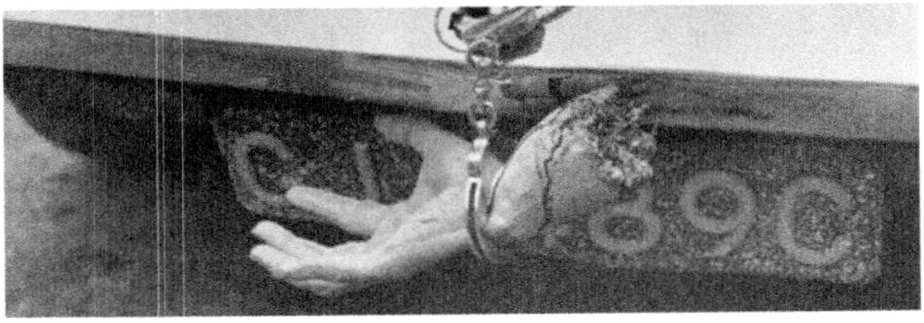

As mentioned earlier, the cast list is a mild cheat, since the three big horror stars are never together in the same scene. The movie itself is rather disjointed in parts, but at least it got Amicus back into the right ball park.

THE HOUSE THAT DRIPPED BLOOD (1970)

CREDITS: Producers: Max J. Rosenberg/Milton Subotsky; Director: Peter Duffell; Screenplay: Robert Bloch; Cinematographer: Ray Parslow; Editor: Peter Tanner; Production Company: Amicus.

CAST: Christopher Lee, Peter Cushing, Jon Pertwee, Nyree Dawn Porter, John Bennett, Denholm Elliott, Ingrid Pitt, Tom Adams, Joss Ackland, Joanna Dunham, Robert Lang, Chloe Franks.

SUMMARY**:** A movie star is missing and an investigator is on the case. It turns out the house the star was staying in has a mysterious history. The stories of recent residents soon unfold. Author Denholm Elliott, who had been living there, created a fictional killer for a novel ... but was the character really fictional?

Peter Cushing was a resident too. He found the image of a lost love in the local wax museum, but got more than he bargained for. When Christopher Lee lived there, he was deathly afraid of his young daughter, and with good reason! And finally, horror film star Jon Pertwee plans to stay in the house while he plays a vampire in his latest movie...but then he becomes one for real. There's a nice in-joke with a vampire cape that says "Property of Shepperton Studios!" And, of course, it's always a treat to see Ingrid.

The framing device for the film ends with the skeptical investigator visiting the house and getting an unpleasant surprise. And just before the closing credits, we learn the real secret of the house is that it takes on the personalities of its inhabitants!

COMMENTS: This film marks a successful return to the Amicus omnibus formula for the first time since *Torture Garden. The House That Dripped Blood* is perhaps the best example of the mixture of horror and humor that became an Amicus trademark. Jon Pertwee is perfect as the self-absorbed horror star. And real horror stars Peter Cushing and Christopher Lee give their usual fine performances.

I, MONSTER (1971)

CREDITS: Producers: Max J. Rosenberg/Milton Subotsky; Director: Stephen Weeks, Screenplay: Milt Subotsky; Cinematographer: Moray Grant; Editor: Peter Tanner; Production Company: Amicus.

CAST: Christopher Lee, Peter Cushing, Mike Raven, George Merritt, Richard Hurndall, Kenneth J. Warren, Susan Jameson.

SUMMARY: Don't for a moment get confused and think that the following plot sounds an awful lot like *Dr. Jekyll and Mr. Hyde*. That story was filmed so many times that Amicus felt it would be hard to find financial backing for anther remake. So the plot for *I, Monster* is totally different. Chris Lee plays Dr. Marlowe who, not unlike Dr. Jekyll, conducts experiments that turn him into the monstrous Mr. Blake, not to be confused with Mr. Hyde. In an amazing coincidence, Dr. Marlowe's face also takes on a frightening appearance, complete with snaggly teeth, an ape-like, puffed-out area surrounding the mouth and dissipated sagging eye pouches.

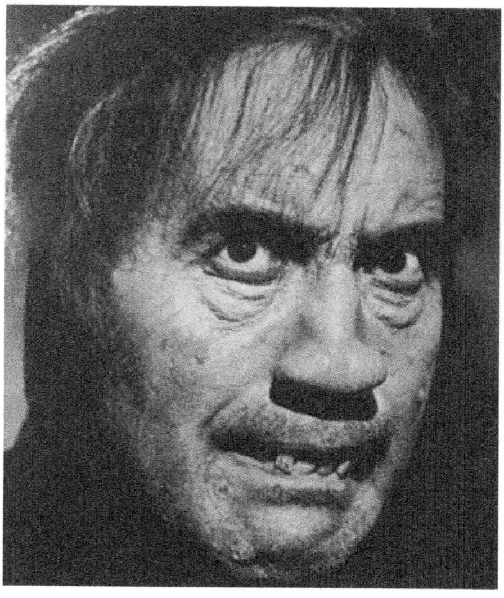

COMMENTS: The main reason to see this film is to catch Christopher Lee in what amounts to the Amicus version of *Jekyll and Hyde* in everything but name. Mike Raven was an unfortunate choice for the movie, but Peter Cushing gives his usual excellent performance.

The film is fine, but I still find it difficult to watch some parts of it because the background seems to be constantly in motion. As mentioned earlier, this was because of Milt Subotsky's original plans to release the film in an untested form of 3-D that necessitated too much camera movement. In addition, the script is rather slow because it sticks so closely to the original story. The screenplay is much like the old *Classics Illustrated* edition of *Jekyll and Hyde*. I remember, as a kid, being very scared in some parts of the comic book but ... dare I say it ... bored in others. I feel much the same about the film, even though I enjoyed spending time roaming the sets at Shepperton.

WHAT BECAME OF JACK AND JILL (1972)

CREDITS: Producers: Max J. Rosenberg/Milton Subotsky; Director: Bill Bain; Screenplay: Roger Marshall; Cinematographer: Gerry Turpin; Editor: Peter Tanner; Production Company: Amicus.

CAST: Vanessa Howard, Paul Nicholas, Mona Washbourne, George Benson, George A. Cooper, Peter Copley.

SUMMARY: Despite attempts to pretend this was a horror film in the advertising ("Jack and Jill Are Out to Kill ... To Grandmother's House They Go.") this is just a nasty little tale about two spoiled kids who want to get grandma out of the way so they can get their hands on her money.

They convince the old girl that the youth of the world are calling for death to seniors as part of their agenda.

COMMENTS: Amicus had been successful producing teen musicals with lots of famous rock acts belting out their hits.

They had also been successful with horror movies. So why would the studio now decide to make a film about teens that featured a loud rock music soundtrack but no famous performers? Even with sexy Vanessa Howard as one of the leads, the movie just didn't make much sense.

Asian posters made it look like a first rate horror flick.

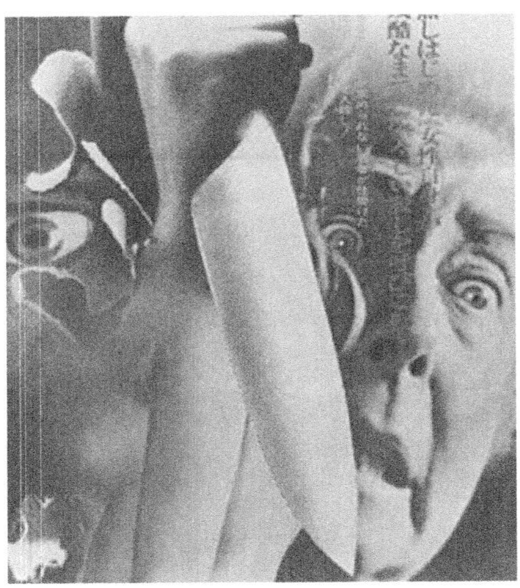

Not surprisingly, the movie failed at the box office.

TALES FROM THE CRYPT (1972)

CREDITS: Producers: Max J. Rosenberg/Milton Subotsky; Director: Freddie Francis; Screenplay: Milton Subotsky; Cinematographer: Norman Warwick; Editor: Teddy Darvas; Production Company: Amicus.

CAST: Peter Cushing, Joan Collins, Ralph Richardson, Patrick Magee, Ian Hendry, Richard Greene, Nigel Patrick, Barbara Murray, Robert Hutton.

SUMMARY: Even though Ralph Richardson doesn't look anything like the EC comics crypt keeper, the stories he helps introduce are very good. Joan Collins gives a Christmas gift of death to her husband, but a homicidal Santa escapes from an asylum and turns the tables on her.

Next, Ian Hendry, trying to find help after a car crash, can't figure out why everyone is so frightened of him, that is until he ... and we ... find out he's a corpse. Speaking of corpses, in the next segment kindly old Peter Cushing falls victim to evil neighbors. But death doesn't stop him from getting his revenge. This tale is followed by one starring Richard Greene, with Greene dying and his wife having her wish that he be brought back to life granted ... but in a very painful way. Somehow Milt managed to work his favorite mechanical hand into the coffin scene.

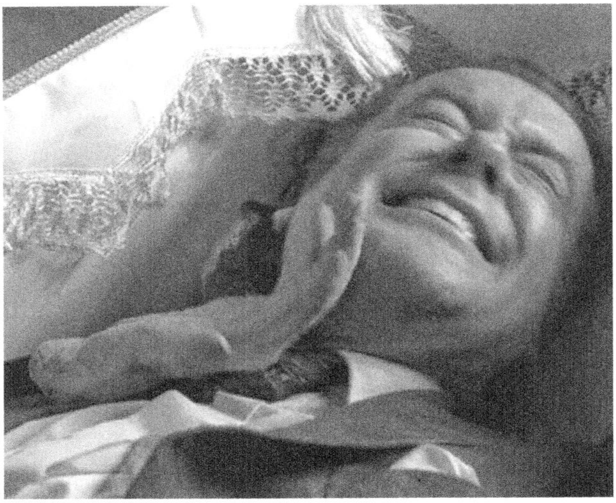

In the final story, Patrick Magee leads the ill-treated residents of a home for the blind in a revolt that takes horrific revenge on the man responsible.

COMMENTS: From this point on, Amicus would stay with its strengths. *Tales from the Crypt* was the studio's first attempt to mine the treasure trove of stories from EC Comics for an anthology film. Al Feldstein, who together with William Gaines was responsible for EC comics, reportedly felt Richardson was wrong for the part of the crypt keeper and apparently had some concerns about the way a couple of the stories were adapted. But the movie benefits from an especially strong performance by Peter Cushing and a well-balanced distribution of star-power elsewhere as well.

ASYLUM (1972)

CREDITS: Producers: Max J. Rosenberg/Milton Subotsky; Director: Roy Ward Baker; Screenplay: Robert Bloch; Cinematographer: Denys Coop; Editor: Peter Tanner; Production Company: Amicus.

CAST: Peter Cushing, Herbert Lom, Patrick Magee, Robert Powell, Barry Morse, Britt Ekland, Barbara Parkins, Charlotte Rampling, Richard Todd, Sylvia Syms.

SUMMARY: The framing story has a psychiatrist showing up at an asylum where he's interviewing to replace a doctor who had a breakdown and is now one of the patients. The new arrival is told he'll get the job if he can figure out which one of the patients is the disturbed doctor. In one segment, Barbara Parkins relates the story of a plot to murder the wife of her lover. In another, Barry Morse of *The Fugitive* fame, is a former tailor who recounts what happened when he made a suit out of a mysterious fabric for Peter Cushing.

Barry Morse and Peter Cushing

Meanwhile, Charlotte Rampling blames her "mirror image" Britt Ekland for the death of her brother.

Also among the inmates, we find Herbert Lom who reveals he's been experimenting with bringing miniature mannequins to life. Yes, it's a strange crew alright.

COMMENTS: This film has a twist ending that viewers won't soon forget.

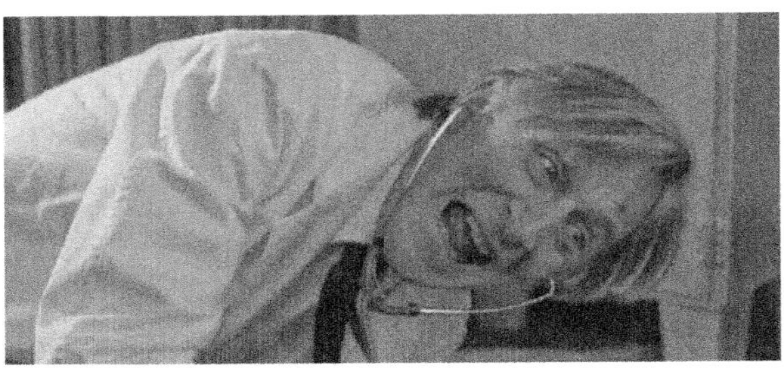

It includes one of the most over-the-top maniacal laughter scenes since Bramwell Fletcher went off the deep end in the original *Mummy* (1932.)

AND NOW THE SCREAMING STARTS! (1973)

CREDITS: Producers: Max J. Rosenberg/Milton Subotsky; Director: Roy Ward Baker; Screenplay: Roger Marshal; Cinematographer: Denys Coop; Editor: Peter Tanner; Production Company: Amicus.

CAST: Peter Cushing, Ian Ogilvy, Stephanie Beacham, Herbert Lom, Patrick Magee, Guy Rolfe, Geoffrey Whitehead, Rosalie Crutchley, Gillian Lind, Sally Harrison, Janet Key

SUMMARY: Ian Ogilvy brings the lovely Stephanie Beacham to his ancestral home, but barely has their life together started than it's interrupted by ghostly goings-on.

It's up to Peter Cushing to try to unravel the mystery behind a family curse.

COMMENTS: It's interesting to see Amicus trying its hand at gothic horror. Speaking of "hand," Milt managed to do it again. This time the mechanical hand creeps along the upstairs mansion floor.

The cast brings together the best of the "Old School" like Herbert Lom and Patrick Magee, with Ogilvy and Beacham.

It's an unusual treat to see Hammer favorite Oakley Court "starring" in an Amicus film. In the opening of *And Now the Screaming Starts* the mansion is shot from the side of the Thames that eventually leads to Hammer's old Bray Studios property further down the road.

VAULT OF HORROR (1973)

CREDITS: Producers: Max J. Rosenberg/Milton Subotsky; Director: Roy Ward Baker; Screenplay: Milton Subotsky; Cinematographer: Denys Coop; Editor: Oswald Hafenrichter; Production Company: Amicus.

CAST: Curt Jürgens, Tom Baker, Denholm Elliott, Dawn Adams, Daniel Massey, Anna Massey, Terry-Thomas, Glynis Johns.

SUMMARY: An elevator takes several men to the bottom of an office building, where it appears they will be forced to spend some time together. They find themselves engaged in conversation about dreams. As it turns out, each man has a recurring nightmare.

The first dream torments Daniel Massey. He visits his sister (played by real-life sister Anna Massey) in a town where normal people lock themselves in at night to avoid wandering vampires. In the next dream, Terry-Thomas is a neatness freak who drives his new bride Glynis Johns crazy with his "A place for everything and everything in its place" demands. Glynis finds a unique way of dealing with the problem ... one that shows she's finally learned to follow her husband's advice.

The next recurring dream belongs to Curt Jürgens, a magician who will do anything to get his hands on new tricks for his act. In the dream he's killed by the rope trick he steals. Meanwhile, Michael Craig's nightmare involves a fake plot to be buried alive and collect some insurance. In his dream, Michael winds up buried alright, but not alive! And finally Tom "Dr. Who" Baker, a painter cheated by art dealers, dreams his paintings are like voodoo dolls ... he can use paintings of his enemies to destroy them. The only problem is, the mysterious power can work on all of his paintings, including a self-portrait.

COMMENTS: The film is good in parts, but overall it's a disappointment compared to the earlier Amicus EC offering, *Tales from the Crypt*. EC's William Gaines apparently wasn't too pleased with it, as this marked the end of the Amicus/EC association.

FROM BEYOND THE GRAVE (1973)

CREDITS: Producers: Max J. Rosenberg/Milton Subotsky; Director: Kevin Connor; Screenplay: Raymond Christodoulou, Robin Clarke; Cinematographer: Alan Hume; Editor: John Ireland; Production Company: Amicus.

CAST: Peter Cushing, Ian Bannen, Donald Pleasence, Angela Pleasence, Diana Dors, Ian Carmichael, Nyree Dawn Porter, Ian Ogilvy, Lesley-Anne Down.

SUMMARY: It isn't nice to try to cheat Peter Cushing! That's the message in this neat little film that uses Peter's antiques shop as a framing device to tell the stories of several visitors to the cluttered store. The first is David Warner who cons Cushing into selling him an antique mirror for much less than it's worth. But, of course, Warner doesn't know that the mirror comes with a little something extra that will turn him into a killer.

Next, Ian Bannen steals a medal from the shop and gets involved with Donald Pleasence and his daughter Angela (father and daughter in real life too.) Before it's all over, Ian's wife Diana Dors will die and Ian will get an unpleasant surprise just as he's about to remarry. Angela Pleasence uses Ian's image on the cake like a voodoo doll, cutting through its head to produce a fatal wound on the real Ian.

The next person unwise enough to try to cheat Peter is Ian Carmichael, who switches price tags on a snuff box and winds up getting his comeuppance. That's followed by Ian Ogilvy, who is actually an honest man. He buys an antique door and when left alone in the front of the shop, he doesn't take any money from the till. However, when Ogilvy takes his purchase home, he and his wife find themselves fighting the door's evil powers. They win, but only because Cushing has counted the money in the till and found it to be correct. At the very end of the film, a thief breaks into Peter's store and finds the seemingly frail old man is anything but!

COMMENTS: This was the last omnibus film to be released under the Amicus banner and it's nice to be able to say that the studio ended its contribution to the genre on a high note. Visiting Amicus at the time this film was being shot, I couldn't help but notice how efficient the company had become in producing these anthology films on tight budgets and tight schedules.

MADHOUSE (1974)

CREDITS: Producers: Max J. Rosenberg/Milton Subotsky; Director: Jim Clark; Screenplay: Greg Morrison, Ken Levison; Cinematographer: Ray Parslow; Editor: Clive Smith; Production Company: Amicus.

CAST: Vincent Price, Peter Cushing, Adrienne Corri, Robert Quarry, Michael Parkinson, Linda Hayden, Natasha Pyne.

SUMMARY: Vincent Price plays a famous horror movie actor (not too big a casting stretch) who was known for years for his role of "Dr. Death." However, his career is interrupted when his girlfriend is killed and he winds up as a suspect. After spending time in a mental hospital, Price is about to revive the "Dr. Death" character when a new series of murders begins. Once again, Vincent is the main suspect and the rest of the film plays out like an old fashioned horror/mystery as he tries to find the real killer.

COMMENTS: Price and Cushing really make this film.

Watching them together on the screen you can get a sense of the fun they're having. Watching from behind the scenes, as I was, it was even more evident. Using clips from Vincent's old movies was undoubtedly an economy move, but seeing Boris Karloff and Basil Rathbone in the same movie with Vincent and Peter added to the nostalgic atmosphere.

THE BEAST MUST DIE (1974)

CREDITS: Producers: Max J. Rosenberg/Milton Subotsky; Director: Paul Annett; Screenplay: Michael Winder; Cinematographer: Jack Hildyard; Editor: Peter Tanner; Production Company: Amicus.

CAST: Peter Cushing, Anton Diffring, Calvin Lockhart, Michael Gambon, Marlene Clark, Charles Gray, Tom Chadbon, Ciaran Madden.

SUMMARY: A wealthy hunter dreams of catching a prey truly worthy of his talents. He suspects one of several people of being a werewolf. So, he invites them over and then waits ... and watches. It doesn't take long before our suspect list starts dwindling and the movie takes on an *And Then There Were None* atmosphere. Anton Diffring, who is in charge of the surveillance system that guards the mansion and the grounds, is among those facing a messy end.

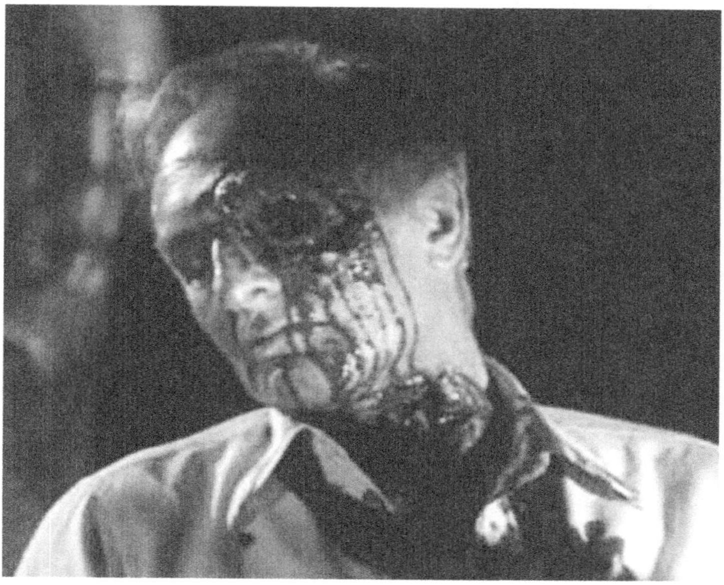

Even after the hokey "Werewolf Break" near the end of the

film, there are some surprises to come.

COMMENTS: This was the final official Amicus horror film and it proved to be a disappointment. Its reliance on cheesy action, zoom shots and a jazz score made it seem more like one of the last "Fu Manchu" offerings from Harry Alan Towers. However, for fans who know Michael Gambon primarily from his appearances in the Harry Potter films and television programs, catching him in this film is a must!

It's fun to see Gambon here as a typical young man of the seventies, bell-bottoms and all!

THE LAND THAT TIME FORGOT (1975

CREDITS: Producers: John Dark/Max J. Rosenberg/Milton Subotsky; Director: Kevin Connor; Screenplay: James Cawthorne, Michael Moorcock; Cinematographer: Alan Hume; Editor: John Ireland; Production Company: Amicus.

CAST: Doug McClure, John McEnery, Susan Penhaligon, Anthony Ainley, Keith Barron, Godfrey James, Declan Mulholland, Bobby Parr, Colin Farrell.

SUMMARY: During World War I the Germans sink a British ship. But little do they know that Doug McClure is aboard. Rescued, Doug and his cohorts fight the Germans at every turn even as the ship mistakenly heads for a lost land filled with dangerous dinosaurs and cavemen.

And, oh yes, there are volcanic eruptions to be dealt with. A World War, dinosaurs, cavemen...a lesser man would be daunted, but to Doug it's all in a day's work.

COMMENTS: Milton Subotsky had long wanted to do a film

version of an Edgar Rice Burroughs adventure that the younger set could enjoy and *The Land That Time Forgot* fit the bill.

Yes, the "special effects" consisted mostly of rear screen projection and very cheesy "dinosaurs."

But ask any adult who saw this movie as a child and they'll tell you they still remember it fondly.

AT THE EARTH'S CORE (1976)

CREDITS: Producers: John Dark/Max J. Rosenberg/Milton Subotsky; Director: Kevin Connor; Screenplay: Milton Subotsky; Cinematographer: Alan Hume; Editors: John Ireland, Barry Peters; Production Company: Amicus.

CAST: Doug McClure, Peter Cushing, Caroline Munro, Cy Grant, Keith Barron, Godfrey James, Sean Lynch, Helen Gill, Anthony Verner, Bobby Parr.

SUMMARY: Doug McClure joins Peter Cushing on a trip to the center of the earth in Peter's giant drilling machine. There are the usual problems along the way, as when director Kevin Connor tells Peter and Doug to throw themselves against the sets while he has cinematographer Alan Hume move the camera from side to side to signal that the drill has run into turbulence. To no one's great surprise, the underground world Peter and Doug reach contains dinosaurs and cavemen. To the delight of all the older boys in the audience, it's also the home of lovely Caroline Munro.

There's a touching scene between Doug and Caroline just before he must return to the surface, but apparently no one alerted the Academy of Motion Picture Arts and Sciences, since I don't recall either of them being nominated.

COMMENTS: The *Land That Time Forgot* was a hit, so it was inevitable that there would be another film aimed at the younger set. This time around everything was played strictly for laughs, but there was something for everyone. Moms who took the kids to see it could enjoy Doug McClure, dads could enjoy Caroline Munro, and the kids could enjoy the dinosaurs. It should be noted, though, that they looked even worse than in the first film. One "monster" is a guy wearing a rubber "Godzilla-type" suit from the neck down and sporting a head that's the spitting image of the muppet character "Sam the Eagle."

At the Earth's Core was the last official Amicus film ... the Rosenberg/Subotsky partnership had already fallen apart by the time it was released.

POST AMICUS

Since Milton Subotsky and Max Rosenberg were no longer together, American International is the logo looming large in the credits for *The People That Time Forgot*. Kevin Connor and John Dark got together with Rosenberg on this 1977 film. Doug McClure is a "Guest Star" on this one, showing up about an hour in and getting killed shortly thereafter. Patrick Wayne handles the leading man chores and it's nice to see Hammer alumni Thorley Walters, David Prowse and Milton Reid getting some work. A special effects award should go to whoever devised the method for keeping Dana Gillespie's breasts from totally spilling out of her cave girl suit.

There was another Doug McClure film after this one, which has the "Amicus Look" because it was produced by John Dark and Kevin Connor, with Connor once again directing. *Warlords of Atlantis* a.k.a. *Warlords of the Deep* was distributed by EMI in 1978. The "monsters," like those in the earlier films, are totally unconvincing. And, when Dark and Connor tried to imitate Subotsky by including "Names" in the cast, it's almost as if they simply opened up a Screen Actors Guild Directory and picked the first names they saw. Dancer Cyd Charisse, who co-starred with Fred Astaire in *Silk Stockings* puts in an appearance here, as does John Ratzenberger, who would later play postal worker Cliff Clavin on the TV show *Cheers*. Speaking of which, by a rather large stretch, the 1979 film *Arabian Adventure*, which also features Ratzenberger, can be considered a kind of great-grandchild of Kevin Connor's Amicus films. Once again, Connor produced it with John Dark and frequent Amicus cinematographer Alan Hume was behind the camera. Christopher Lee and Peter Cushing even appeared in the film, along with Milton Reid of Hammer fame. But other casting was less than inspired, including Mickey Rooney playing a character named Daad El Shur!

Hey, why not Rooney as "El Shur?" After all, Ratzenberger's name is Achmed in this one. You can almost see "Achmed" on a bar stool at "Cheers" confidently holding forth on something he knows nothing about. ("Yeah, not many people know it, but your flying carpets don't actually fly....")

Milton Subotsky remained busy after his partnership with Max Rosenberg fell apart. But, unfortunately, neither of the men managed to duplicate the success of their Amicus days. Milt was at least on the right track when he produced 1977's *The Uncanny*. This was an attempt by Subotsky to find renewed success with the omnibus horror film format. *The Uncanny* was shot in Canada rather than England, but the cast was outstanding. Director Denis Héroux was working with Peter Cushing, Ray Milland, Chloe Franks, Donald Pleasence and Samantha Eggar.

Denis Héroux directs Samantha Eggar

Unfortunately, the overall look and feel of the film just isn't the same as the old Amicus offerings. The framing device here has Peter Cushing trying to convince Ray Milland that cats are evil, supernatural creatures. He tells three stories to get his point across, but that's part of the problem. Subotsky told me back in England that the secret to a good anthology film was having four or five stories, so if a viewer grew bored with one of them he'd know another was coming up shortly. Sadly, other than the Donald Pleasence/Samantha Eggar segment, the three presented here aren't that strong, although the framing story benefits from having two pros like Milland and Cushing.

One other problem with the film: While some of the cats in *The Uncanny* look scary, many others appear to be downright friendly, including Ray Milland's cat who looks like she's on loan from the Meow-Mix commercials!

Subotsky's next film was *Dominique* (aka *Dominique is Dead.*) It had an excellent cast that included Cliff Robertson, Jean Simmons, Jenny Agutter, Ron Moody, Simon Ward, Judy Geeson and Flora Robson. Cliff Robertson wants to get his hands on wife Jean Simmons' money. He finally succeeds in getting her to commit suicide. But then it appears the tables have turned and she's come back to haunt him. Ah, but those of us who've seen this sort of thing many times before know all is not what it seems. This plot would have been perfect as an individual segment of one of the old Amicus omnibus films. The story could have been told in 20 minutes instead of dragging it out to a full length feature that moves at a glacier-like crawl. For years Milton had wanted to make an omnibus horror film aimed at children and he got his chance in 1980 with *The Monster Club*. The film unfortunately failed to find an audience despite a first-rate cast that included Vincent Price, Donald Pleasence, Patrick Magee, Richard Johnson and Britt Ekland, all of whom had worked at Amicus years earlier. There were some pluses for the film, though. It's good to see Britt Ekland, Richard Johnson and Donald Pleasence having some fun in the "Vampire" segment.

Another segment, with the rather silly title "The Humgoo Story," is the one I find most interesting. This tale is almost like Milton Subotsky's homage to his first horror film, *City of the Dead*. It provides a fascinating glimpse into what the 1959 classic might have looked like if it were filmed more than 20 years later and in color! Essentially, Patrick Magee plays the innkeeper role handled by Patricia Jessel in the first film, and Stuart Whitman, like Venetia Stevenson in

City of the Dead, finds himself getting more than he bargained for when he visits a strange village.

Even the timbered village sets Subotsky had constructed for the 1980 movie look strikingly similar to those that represented the village of Whitewood in the 1959 film.

In some ways it seemed things had come full circle.

AFTERWORD

At a time when intelligent horror films of the kind so many of us loved have all but disappeared, an examination of the special people and unique period that produced these classics is long overdue. It seems strange to be in a position where I can remember watching some of these movies being filmed and yet still be around to see new audiences discovering them via video streaming, DVD, etc.

The period of greatest success for Amicus began in 1965. I don't think it's any coincidence that the year was one of the most turbulent in recent history. America was suffering heavy losses in Vietnam and the anti-war movement was gaining ground. There was civil unrest, including the riots in Los Angeles. Meanwhile, Britain initiated a new Race Relations Act in a bid to ease inner city disturbances. Adults on both sides of the pond were confused by the sudden switch to maxi-length hair for men and mini-length skirts for woman. Into this world of jarring change, Milton Subotsky was about to introduce a welcome note of reassurance.

There's a certain type of mystery book that's known in the trade as a "cozy." Agatha Christie's mysteries would be a prime example. There's a feeling of safety and warmth in reading these novels, in part because no matter what the actual setting or time, they really take place in a sort of ageless never-never land that somehow reminds us of more innocent days.

In a way, that's what so many of the Amicus films are like. The Britain depicted in movies like *The House That Dripped Blood* and *From Beyond the Grave* was fast disappearing or already gone by the time they were being shot. As I mentioned earlier, Milton told me he thought of horror films as adult fairy tales. I think he gave his movies this never-never land setting for the same reason.

Strictly speaking, Amicus made only one "Gothic" film in the years it was active, *And Now The Screaming Starts*! But in reality, most of the studio's films could really be considered "Modern Gothic." In traditional gothic, the setting is usually a decaying castle or abbey, but is that really so different from the decaying church and Inn featured in *City of the Dead*? And what about the atmosphere of doom that hangs over *The House That Dripped Blood*?

At the same time, the gothic themes of supernatural retribution are in every Amicus horror film in one form or another. Peter Cushing, ill-treated during his life, gets the ultimate revenge from the grave in *Tales from the Crypt*, greedy Daniel Massey's blood winds up on the wine list in *Vault of Horror*, and everybody who takes advantage of Peter Cushing in *From Beyond the Grave* learns crime doesn't pay. That includes Ian Bannen who gets his just deserts when he bleeds out on his own wedding cake!

Going back over my old notes and tapes and reliving the times that I was able to visit Amicus, I find it hard to believe that it was so long ago.

Time is a funny thing. Although the early rock music

films Amicus produced were successful, and even though the studio found its niche ... without really knowing it ... in 1959 with *City of the Dead*, the real glory days for Amicus lasted only from 1964 to 1974. Even that is stretching it a bit. So, at most we're talking about ten years.

But Milton Subotsky, who'd been working non-stop during that period, didn't have time to stop and think that he was making motion picture history. To be honest, it's only in looking back that I realize how lucky I was to witness part of it. When *The House That Dripped Blood* shows up on TV, I still find the opening shot of the title abode scary, even though I was there with the producer and know it was just a small old gatehouse.

It's the same with *I, Monster*, even though I walked the same streets Chris Lee and Peter Cushing walked in the film and know the impressive buildings were just false fronts. And when I'm watching a scene in *From Beyond the Grave*, part of me remembers the set and what little bits of business were going on. But another part of my brain is able to simply sit back, relax and enjoy the movie.

It's the same when I see someone like Peter Cushing in a film today. I see the *role-playing* Peter Cushing (watching a film being shot is almost always like watching kids play-acting, since you're not seeing exactly what the camera is seeing from the angle the camera is seeing it, and often the film doesn't really take shape until it's assembled in the editing process.)

I see the *reel* Peter Cushing ... the character in the movie that I'm watching, which he always plays so convincingly. And best of all, I remember the *real* Peter Cushing ... the warm and friendly person who was happy to share stories with my wife and I.

When I said goodbye to Milton Subotsky in 1973, I'm sure he had no idea that within two years he'd be out at

Amicus. And he had no way of knowing how many years he'd have to waste being involved in suits and countersuits. Despite it all he still managed to get some projects going that he enjoyed, but there were disappointments as well, and there was never anything that really rivaled the Amicus days. Milton died in 1991, Max Rosenberg in 2004.

Fortunately for all of us, when it comes to Amicus we have much more than just memories. We have a celluloid history of some of the best films from the famed glory days of British horror. They're always available for those of us who wish to take a trip back in time to the relatively innocent days of our youth, before the term "horror movie" became synonymous with "slasher flick." And somehow it's comforting to know that the Amicus films we loved so long ago are now being enjoyed by whole new generations.

BY THE SAME AUTHOR:

The only two books exclusively devoted to the Horror films and Mysteries produced by the legendary Republic Studios!

ALSO BY BRIAN MCFADDEN

The First-Ever Guides to Budget LPs of the Fifties & Sixties!

Note: The years that appear in connection with the films mentioned in this book generally refer to the release dates. The production dates differ. The images in this reference/research work are used herein for historic and scholarly purposes under the Fair Use provisions of the United States copyright laws. While every effort has been made to provide proper acknowledgement where it is due, in the event of any inadvertent omissions we shall be pleased to correct them in future editions.

Printed in Great Britain
by Amazon

33859831R00159